IDIOT'S
GUIDES.
AS EASY AS IT GETS!

W9-CFG-942

Microsoft®
Excel® 2013

by Michael Miller

ALPHA

A member of Penguin Group (USA) Inc.

ALPHA BOOKS

Published by Penguin Group (USA) Inc.

Penguin Group (USA) Inc., 375 Hudson Street, New York, New York 10014, USA • Penguin Group (Canada), 90 Eglinton Avenue East, Suite 700, Toronto, Ontario M4P 2Y3, Canada (a division of Pearson Penguin Canada Inc.) • Penguin Books Ltd., 80 Strand, London WC2R 0RL, England • Penguin Ireland, 25 St. Stephen's Green, Dublin 2, Ireland (a division of Penguin Books Ltd.) • Penguin Group (Australia), 250 Camberwell Road, Camberwell, Victoria 3124, Australia (a division of Pearson Australia Group Pty. Ltd.) • Penguin Books India Pvt. Ltd., 11 Community Centre, Panchsheel Park, New Delhi—110 017, India • Penguin Group (NZ), 67 Apollo Drive, Rosedale, North Shore, Auckland 1311, New Zealand (a division of Pearson New Zealand Ltd.) • Penguin Books (South Africa) (Pty.) Ltd., 24 Sturdee Avenue, Rosebank, Johannesburg 2196, South Africa • Penguin Books Ltd., Registered Offices: 80 Strand, London WC2R 0RL, England

International Standard Book Number: 978-1-61564-454-4
Library of Congress Catalog Card Number: 2013952988

16 15 14   8 7 6 5 4 3 2 1

Interpretation of the printing code: The rightmost number of the first series of numbers is the year of the book's printing; the rightmost number of the second series of numbers is the number of the book's printing. For example, a printing code of 14-1 shows that the first printing occurred in 2014.

Note: This publication contains the opinions and ideas of its author. It is intended to provide helpful and informative material on the subject matter covered. It is sold with the understanding that the author and publisher are not engaged in rendering professional services in the book. If the reader requires personal assistance or advice, a competent professional should be consulted. The author and publisher specifically disclaim any responsibility for any liability, loss, or risk, personal or otherwise, which is incurred as a consequence, directly or indirectly, of the use and application of any of the contents of this book.

Most Alpha books are available at special quantity discounts for bulk purchases for sales promotions, premiums, fundraising, or educational use. Special books, or book excerpts, can also be created to fit specific needs. For details, write: Special Markets, Alpha Books, 375 Hudson Street, New York, NY 10014.

Trademarks: All terms mentioned in this book that are known to be or are suspected of being trademarks or service marks have been appropriately capitalized. Alpha Books and Penguin Group (USA) Inc. cannot attest to the accuracy of this information. Use of a term in this book should not be regarded as affecting the validity of any trademark or service mark.

Publisher: Mike Sanders

Executive Managing Editor: Billy Fields

Senior Acquisitions Editor: Brook Farling

Development Editorial Supervisor: Christy Wagner

Senior Production Editor: Janette Lynn

Senior Web/Graphic Designer: William Thomas

Indexer: Johnna VanHoose Dinse

Proofreader: Laura Caddell

Contents

Working with Worksheets 105

Formatting Worksheets and Workbooks 123

Working with Ranges 139

Using Formulas and Functions 159

Creating Charts 183

Adding Graphics 213

Working with Tables 225

Working with PivotTables

Analyzing Data

Printing

Sharing and Collaborating

Glossary

Keyboard Shortcuts

Index

Introduction

If you work with any numbers or data, chances are you work with Microsoft Excel. Excel is the spreadsheet program included in Microsoft Office that lets you input, store, and manipulate text and (especially) numbers in all sorts of ways. It's an essential application for work and home productivity. At work, Excel enables you to create sales projections, manage budgets and forecasts, and do all manner of number crunching, from simple to advanced. At home, Excel helps you manage home budgets, create shopping lists, keep track of investments, and work with just about anything else you can put in rows and columns.

The challenge comes in trying to figure out exactly *how* to use Excel to do what you want to do. Excel is a very powerful program with tons of built-in features, but it isn't always intuitive which of those features you need to use or how you should use them. That's where this book comes in.

Idiot's Guides: Microsoft® Excel® 2013 presents the information you need to get the most out of Excel in a series of easy-to-follow, step-by-step visual lessons. Just follow the steps and accompanying screenshots as you follow along on your computer, and you'll be using Excel like a pro in no time. Using Excel really is easy when you know what to do and how to do it.

Special Thanks to the Technical Reviewer

Idiot's Guides: Microsoft® Excel® 2013 was reviewed by an expert who double-checked the accuracy of what you'll learn here, to help us ensure this book gives you everything you need to know about this useful program. Special thanks are extended to J. Boyd Nolan.

Acknowledgments

Thanks to everyone at Alpha Books involved with taking this project from concept to printed book, including but not limited to Brook Farling, Christy Wagner, and William Thomas. Thanks also to technical editor J. Boyd Nolan, who helped ensure the technical accuracy of the information on these pages. I dedicate this book to my grandkids Alethia, Collin, Hayley, Judah, and Lael, who are all too young to have any idea what a spreadsheet is. Good for them. —Michael

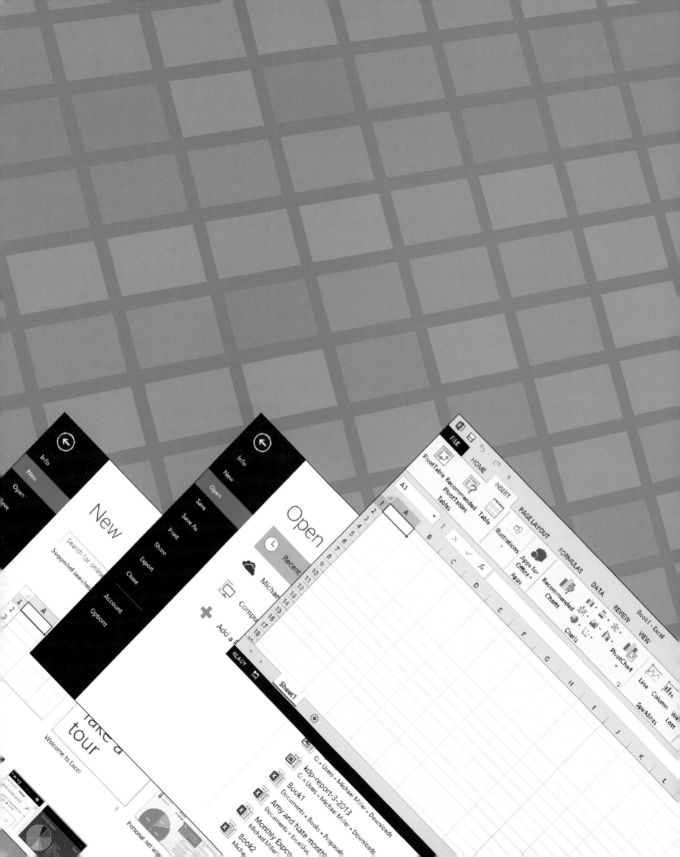

Chapter 1

Getting Started with Excel 2013

Microsoft Excel is a spreadsheet program. And just what is a spreadsheet? It's simply a giant list that can contain just about any type of data you can think of—text, numbers, dates—you name it. You can take any of the numbers in the list and use them to calculate new numbers. You can sort the items in the list, pretty them up, and print just the important points in a report. You can even analyze what the items in the list mean and express them visually in a pie, line, or bar chart.

With Microsoft Excel's spreadsheets, you can do all kinds of number-crunching activities on your computer, from personal budgets to sophisticated "what-if" analyses. It's a matter of entering your data into the cells of the spreadsheet and then using Excel's various features and functions to work with those numbers.

As you might already know, Excel is part of the Microsoft Office suite of applications. (Office also includes Word, PowerPoint, Outlook, and other productivity apps.) The latest version of Excel is Excel 2013, and it's available in both traditional desktop software and cloud-based online versions.

In This Chapter

- Learning all about Microsoft Excel 2013
- Touring the online Excel Web App
- Creating new spreadsheets
- Saving your work
- Opening a previously created spreadsheet
- Changing how you view your spreadsheet
- Personalizing the Ribbon and Quick Access Toolbar

Exploring Excel 2013

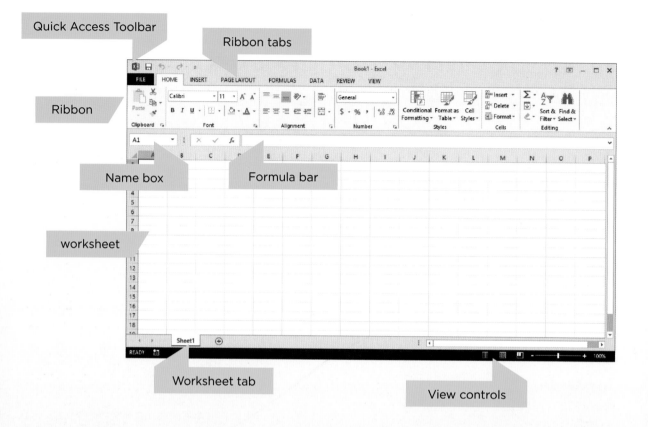

Quick Access Toolbar

Ribbon tabs

Ribbon

Name box

Formula bar

worksheet

Worksheet tab

View controls

Excel is like all Windows applications in that the current document is surrounded by the trappings of the application itself. All the application functions and commands are located in the Ribbon that stretches across the top of the screen. The Ribbon is comprised of multiple tabs, each of which is dedicated to a specific type of operation—Insert, Page Layout, Formulas, and so forth.

Above the Ribbon is a Quick Access Toolbar that contains some of Excel's most frequently used commands. This toolbar is customizable, so you can put your favorite commands here for quick access.

Beneath the Ribbon is a row of useful navigational items. This row includes the Name box, which displays the name of the currently selected cell, and the Formula bar, which displays the contents of the current cell. Between the two is a set of controls you can use to accept or reject entries in the Formula bar or insert specific functions.

The **Home** tab contains Excel's most-used controls for entering, editing, and formatting data.

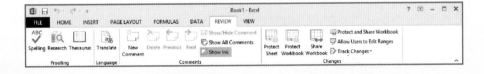

The **Insert** tab contains controls for adding various items to a spreadsheet.

The **Page Layout** tab houses controls for formatting the look and feel of a spreadsheet.

The **Formulas** tab is used to create and edit formulas and functions.

The **Data** tab contains tools for analyzing spreadsheet data.

The **Review** tab contains tools for managing spreadsheet changes.

The **View** tab enables you to change how you view your spreadsheet.

Exploring the Excel Web App

In addition to the traditional Excel desktop app, Microsoft offers a web-based version of Excel dubbed the Excel Web App. The Excel Web App contains a subset of features found on the desktop version. (This book is written on the desktop version of Microsoft Excel 2013 so although most of the instructions in this book also apply to the Excel Web App, be aware that some do not.) In particular, the Excel Web App lacks sophisticated page layout controls and the capability to perform complex data analysis. Even with these limitations, many users find the Excel Web App sufficient for everyday use.

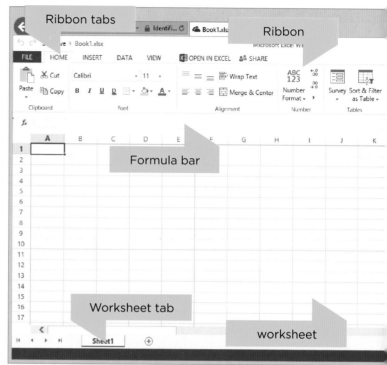

One of the chief benefits of using the Excel Web App is that you can easily share spreadsheets with other users. If people from different locations are working on the same project, each can access the web-based spreadsheet and make changes their collaborators see in real time, or as they make them.

You access the Excel Web App (and all the other Office Web Apps) at skydrive.live.com. Log in with your Microsoft account. You can then import spreadsheet files you've created with the desktop version to the online version, download web files to your computer, and create new spreadsheet files.

> **Note**
>
> Microsoft offers other Office Web Apps for Word, PowerPoint, and OneNote. (There's also a web-based version of Outlook, separate from the Office Web Apps.) These web-based applications operate in the *cloud,* an amalgamation of remote servers hosted online. All the apps and their data are stored in the cloud rather than on your computer.

SkyDrive is Microsoft's web-based storage service. On SkyDrive, files are stored in online folders. To open a spreadsheet file, click to display the contents of a folder and then click to open the file.

To upload an existing Excel file from your computer, click **Upload** to display the Open dialog box, and select the file.

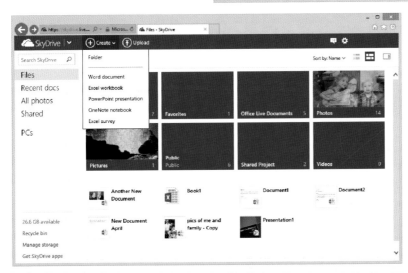

To create a new Excel file, click **Create** on the SkyDrive toolbar, and select **Excel workbook**.

To open an online spreadsheet in the desktop version of Excel, simply click **Open in Excel**.

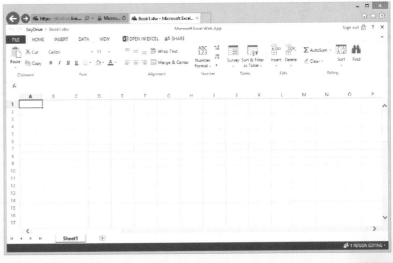

Creating a New Blank Spreadsheet

In Excel, new spreadsheets you create can be completely blank or they can be formatted from predesigned templates. When you want to start completely from scratch, open a blank spreadsheet.

When you first launch Excel, you see a type of welcome screen. The left side of this screen displays your most recent Excel files, and the main part of the screen contains a selection of templates you can use to create new spreadsheets. To launch Excel with an empty spreadsheet, click the **Blank workbook** tile.

> **Note**
>
> In Excel, a spreadsheet file is called a *workbook*. Each workbook can contain multiple sheets, called *worksheets*.

1   To open a blank spreadsheet from within Excel, start by clicking the **File** tab on the Ribbon.

2   When the next screen appears, click **New** in the left-hand navigation sidebar.

3   Click the **Blank workbook** tile. Excel now opens and displays an empty spreadsheet, ready for your input.

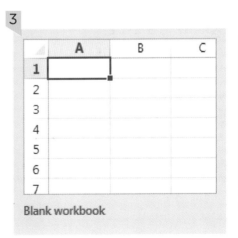

Blank workbook

Creating a New Spreadsheet from a Template

Excel 2013 comes with a number of templates preinstalled. If you have a specific type of spreadsheet in mind, you can get a head start by creating your spreadsheet around one of these templates. Templates include formatting specific to the task at hand, and in some instances, they come with data or formulas already entered, as necessary.

1. From within Excel, click the **File** tab on the Ribbon.

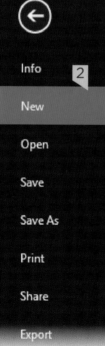

2. When the next screen appears, click **New** in the left-hand navigation sidebar.

> **✎ Note**
>
> When you launch Excel, you're presented with the same screen of templates as you see when you click the **File** tab within the program. If you don't see a template you like, you can search for and download templates from Microsoft's website (microsoft.com).

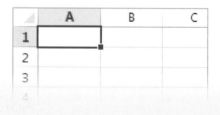

New

Search for online templates

Suggested searches: Budget   Invoice   Calenda

3 You now see a selection of available templates. Scroll down to see more, and click the template you want to use for your new spreadsheet.

4 Clicking a template displays an information box about it. Click **Create** to use this template to create a new spreadsheet.

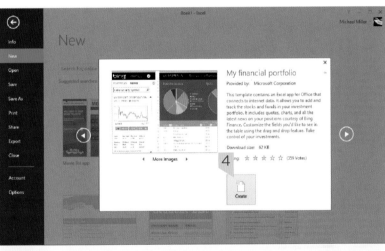

5 To search for additional templates online, enter one or more descriptive words in the **Search for templates online** box, and press **Enter**. Excel will display templates that match your search. Click a category from the list on the right to narrow down the selection, and click the template you'd like to use.

Saving Your Spreadsheet

When you create a new spreadsheet in the Excel desktop program, you must save the file to preserve your data. The first time you save a spreadsheet, you have to name the file. You should continue to save the file as you work on it to avoid losing any data you've input.

When you work with the Excel Web App online, your work is automatically saved to the cloud as you make changes to a spreadsheet. No manual file saving is necessary.

1 From within Excel, click the **File** tab on the Ribbon.

2 Click **Save As** from the sidebar.

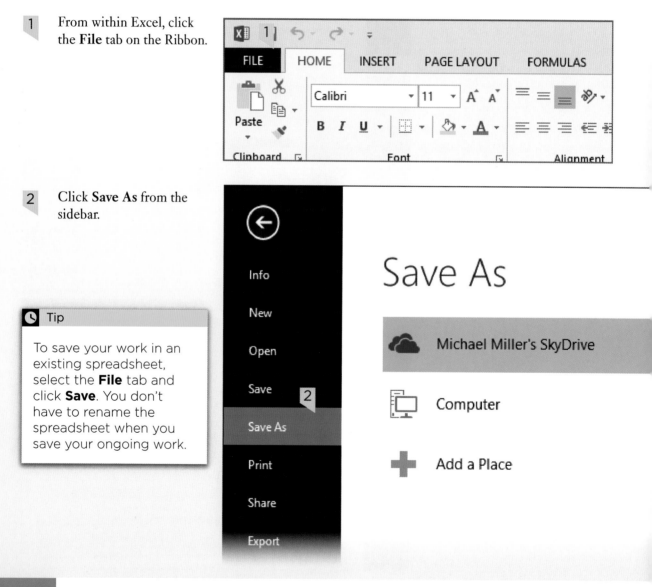

> **Tip**
>
> To save your work in an existing spreadsheet, select the **File** tab and click **Save**. You don't have to rename the spreadsheet when you save your ongoing work.

3 You can save an Excel file locally on your computer's hard drive or online with Microsoft SkyDrive. To save a file to your computer, click **Computer**. To save a file to SkyDrive online, click **SkyDrive**.

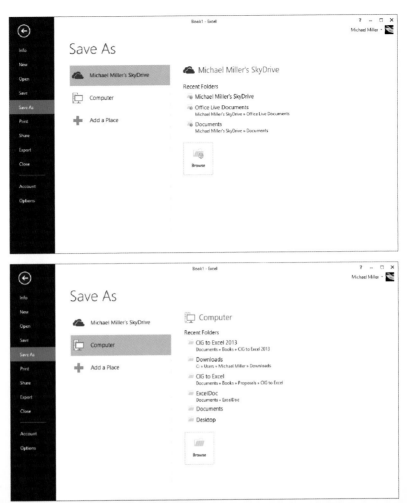

4 Select a location for this file from the **Recent Folders** list, or click the **Browse** button to select a different location.

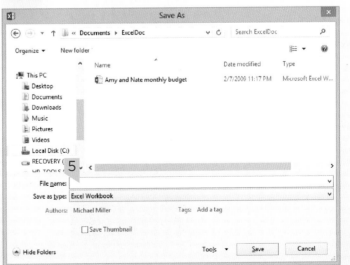

5 When the **Save As** dialog box appears, enter a name for this file in the **File name** box, and click **Save**.

Opening an Existing Spreadsheet

After you've saved a spreadsheet, it's easy to reopen it for additional editing.

1   From within Excel, click the **File** tab on the Ribbon.

2   Click **Open** in the sidebar.

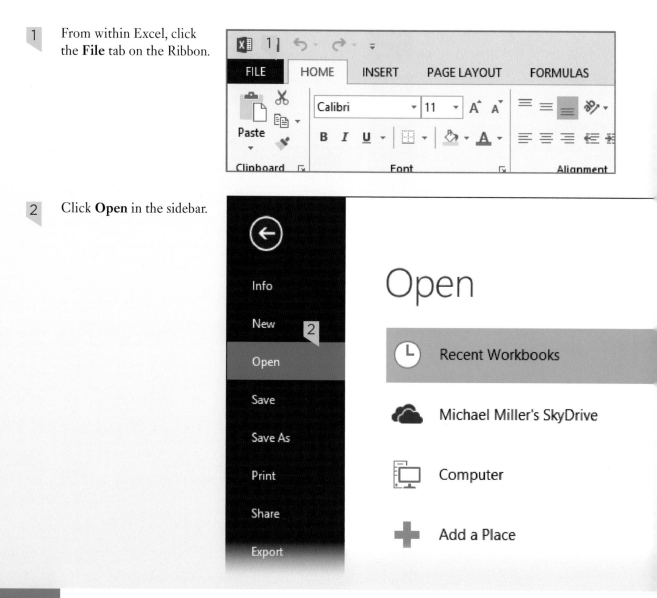

3 To open a recently edited file, click **Recent Workbooks** and then click the file you want to open from the list.

4 To open a file stored online in SkyDrive, click **SkyDrive** and then select or browse for the location of the file you want to open. Click the file to open it.

5 To open a file stored on your computer, click **Computer** and then select or browse for the location of that file. Click the file to open it.

Changing Views

View tab

Tip

Excel features several view commands at the bottom-right corner of the application window. These include buttons for Normal, Page Layout, and Page Break Preview views, as well as a slider to zoom into or out of the spreadsheet.

You can view an Excel spreadsheet in several different ways. *Normal* view displays the standard rows and columns on-screen. *Page Break Preview* displays all the pages of your document on a single screen so you can review where the page breaks fall. *Page Layout* view is also a type of print preview; use it to see how your document will look on the printed page. In addition, *Custom Views* are any views you've personally created and saved for future use.

To change views, click the **View** tab on the Ribbon. All the view-related controls are there.

To create a custom view, adjust the screen as you like, go to the **View** tab, and click the **Custom Views** button. When the Custom Views dialog box appears, click the **Add** button, and enter a name for this view. Your custom views are listed in the Custom Views dialog box when you click the **Custom Views** button.

To change views, click the **View** tab and then click the view you want—**Normal**, **Page Break Preview**, **Page Layout**, or **Custom Views**.

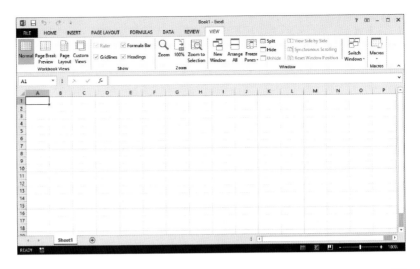

To hide specific screen elements, go to the **Show** section of the **View** tab and uncheck any of the following: **Ruler**, **Formula Bar**, **Gridlines**, or **Headings**.

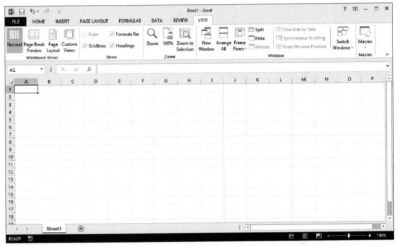

You can make your spreadsheet look bigger or smaller on-screen by zooming into or out of the document. Go to the **Zoom** section of the **View** tab, and click **Zoom**. This displays the Zoom dialog box. Select a magnification (or enter a custom value), and click **OK**. To return to normal (100%) magnification, click **100%** on the **View** tab.

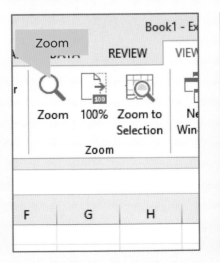

Customizing the Ribbon

You can customize each of the tabs on Excel's Ribbon, removing commands you don't use and adding other commands you find more useful. You can even create new tabs for specific tasks or projects.

1   Right-click on any blank area on the Ribbon, and select **Customize the Ribbon**....

> **⚠ Caution**
>
> Remember to click on a blank area of the Ribbon—not on a Ribbon button—or you'll get options specific to that button, not to the Ribbon itself.

2   When the Excel Options dialog box appears, pull down the **Choose commands from** list and select what commands you want to choose from: Popular Commands (the default), Commands Not in the Ribbon, All Commands, or one of the other options. Then pull down the **Customize the Ribbon** list and select which set of Ribbons you want to customize: Main Tabs (the default), All Tabs, or Tool Tabs (those tabs that only appear when you're performing specific tasks).

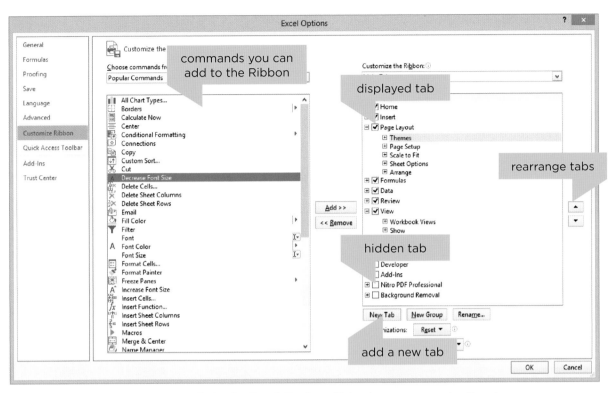

Excel Options

commands you can add to the Ribbon

displayed tab

rearrange tabs

hidden tab

add a new tab

3 There's even more you can do in the Excel Options dialog box to customize Excel:

To hide a tab, uncheck that item in the **Tabs** (right-hand) list. To remove a command from a Ribbon, click the item in the **Tabs** list and then click the **Remove** button.

To change the order of a Ribbon or command, click that item in the **Tabs** list and then click the up or down arrows.

To add a new command to a given Ribbon, highlight the Ribbon in the **Tabs** list, highlight the new command in the **Commands** list, and click the **Add** button.

To add a new tab to the Ribbon, click the **New Tab** button. This adds a "New Tab (Custom)" item to the Tabs list. Click the **Rename…** button to name this tab, and add commands to the tab as explained in step 5. To save the changes you've made, click **OK** when you're done.

Personalizing the Quick Access Toolbar

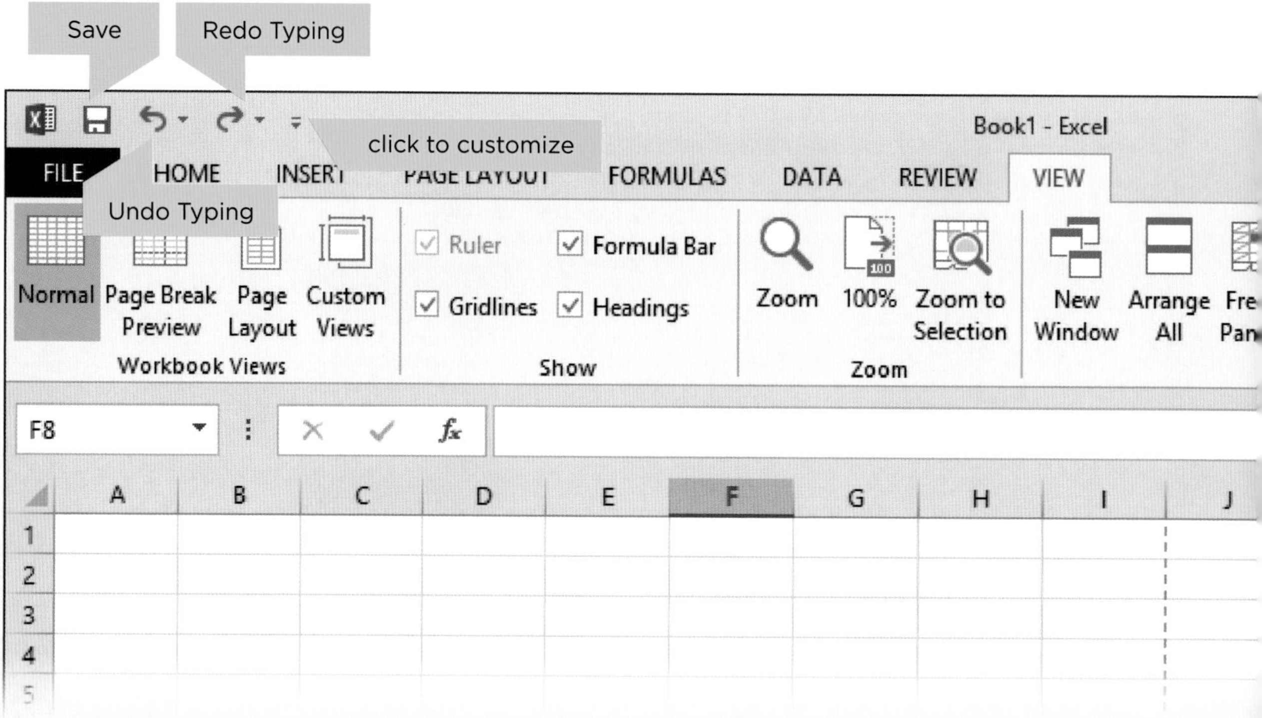

Save

Redo Typing

click to customize

Undo Typing

By default, the Quick Access Toolbar appears *above* the Ribbon. To display it *below* the Ribbon instead, click the down arrow at the end of the toolbar and select **Show Below the Ribbon**.

The Quick Access Toolbar appears above the Ribbon in the Excel window. By default, this toolbar includes three commonly used commands—Save, Undo Typing, and Redo Typing. This is a toolbar that provides quick access to common commands, so you can add your own favorite commands to the toolbar. For example, you might want to add Cut, Copy, and Paste commands for faster editing.

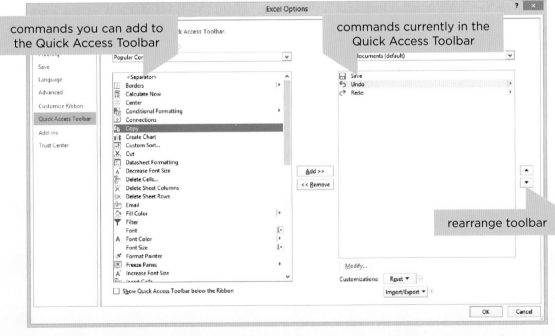

1 To customize the Quick Access Toolbar, click the down arrow at the end of the toolbar to display the list of popular commands. Check those commands you want to display on the toolbar, and uncheck those you don't want to see.

2 To add even more commands to the Quick Access Toolbar, click **More Commands…** to display the Excel Options dialog box. Select a command in the left-hand **Choose commands from** list and then click the **Add** button. To remove a command from the toolbar, select it in the right-hand Customize Quick Access Toolbar list and then click the **Remove** button. Click **OK** when you're done.

Configuring Other Important Options

You can personalize many aspects of Microsoft Excel—the color of the window background, the font displayed in each spreadsheet, how Excel calculates formulas, how often files are saved, and more. Most users accept Excel's default settings, but it's nice to know you can change things if you want.

1. To configure any Excel setting, click the **File** tab and then select **Options**.

2. When the Excel Options dialog box appears, select the tab in the left-hand sidebar for the type of setting you want to configure, and make the desired changes. (The table on the next page details which settings are found on each tab.) Click **OK** when you're done.

Options Tab	Available Settings
General	User Interface options When creating new workbooks (font and view options) Personalize your copy of Microsoft Office (user name, window background color, and Office theme) Start up options
Formulas	Calculation options Working with formulas Error checking Error checking rules
Proofing	AutoCorrect options When correcting spelling in Microsoft Office programs (spell check options)
Save	Save workbooks (file format and AutoRecover options) AutoRecover exceptions for Offline editing options for document management server files Preserve visual appearance of the workbook
Language	Choose Editing Languages Choose Display and Help Languages Choose ScreenTip Language
Advanced	Editing options Cut, copy, and paste Image size and quality Print Chart Display Display options for this workbook/worksheet Formulas When calculating this workbook General Data Lotus compatibility
Customize Ribbon	Customize the Ribbon
Quick Access Toolbar	Customize the Quick Access Toolbar
Add-Ins	View and manage Excel add-ins
Trust Center	View privacy settings

Chapter 2

Entering and Editing Data

A spreadsheet without data is like a farm without animals, a beehive without bees, a library without books. Until you add data, all you have is a bunch of empty cells.

It's the data that makes a spreadsheet useful. That data can be numerical or alphanumeric—that is, numbers or letters. Input what you have to input, and let Excel figure out how to handle it.

Of course, you can edit any data you enter into an Excel spreadsheet. You can even copy data from one cell to another, which is a great way to deal with repeating data. And just in case you need to, you can delete any data you've previously entered.

In This Chapter

- Getting to know the spreadsheet layout
- Entering numbers, date, time, and text
- Editing data in a cell
- Deleting cell data
- Finding and replacing text
- Copying a cell to another location
- Moving a cell from one location to another

Understanding the Spreadsheet Layout

In an Excel spreadsheet (also called a *worksheet*), everything you enter is stored in little boxes called *cells*. Each cell resides in a specific location in a giant grid made of horizontal *rows* and vertical *columns*. Each individual cell represents the intersection of a particular row and column.

Each column in a spreadsheet is identified by a letter (from left to right: A, B, C, and so on). Each row is identified by a number (from top to bottom: 1, 2, 3, and so on). The location of each cell is the combination of its column and row locations. For example, the cell in the upper-left corner of the spreadsheet is in column A and row 1, so its location is signified as A1. The cell to the right of that cell is in column B and row 1, so its location is B1. The cell below A1 is in column A and row 2, so its location is A2.

The location of the selected, or *active*, cell is displayed in the Name box. The contents of the active cell are in the Formula bar, which is next to the Name box. You can enter data into either the active cell or the Formula bar; either approach works just as well.

You can navigate the Excel workspace with your mouse, using the vertical and horizontal scrollbars at the right and the bottom of the window. You can also move around using your keyboard. Keyboard-based navigation is often easier when you're also using your keyboard to input data into the spreadsheet.

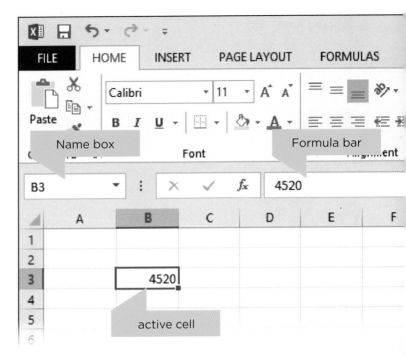

Key or Keyboard Shortcut	Navigation
Up arrow	Move up one cell
Down arrow	Move down one cell
Left arrow	Move left one cell
Right arrow	Move right one cell
Tab	Move right one cell
Shift+Tab	Move left one cell
Home	Move to the left-most cell in the current row
Ctrl+Home	Move to cell A1
Page Down	Move down one screen
Page Up	Move up one screen
Ctrl+Page Down	Move right one screen
Ctrl+Page Up	Move left one screen
Ctrl+End	Move to the last, bottom-right cell in the worksheet

Entering Numbers

Entering any type of data into an Excel spreadsheet is as simple as selecting a cell and typing in the cell using your keyboard. You can also type in the Formula bar after you've selected a cell; whatever you type in the Formula bar is entered into the active cell.

To enter a number, simply move the cursor to the desired cell, using either your mouse or the arrow keys on your keyboard, and begin typing. The number you enter is echoed in the Formula bar. Press **Enter** when you're done. You can cancel your data entry at any time before you press Enter by pressing the **Esc** key.

You can enter numbers in a variety of different formats, including currency and percent. You can then mathematically manipulate the numbers you enter, no matter how they're formatted, using various formulas. (More on using formulas and functions later in the book.)

To enter a whole number, enter only numeric characters (1, 2, 3, and so on). Do not enter letters or special characters.

A1		⋮	✕ ✓ fx	149	

	A	B	C	D	E
1	149				
2					
3					
4					

To enter a decimal number, enter numbers separated by a period (.) as a decimal point, like this: **12.5**.

A1		⋮	✕ ✓ fx	12.5	

	A	B	C	D	E
1	12.5				
2					
3					
4					

To enter a negative number, enter a minus sign (−) in front of the number, like this: **−32**.

SUM		⋮	✕ ✓ fx	-32	

	A	B	C	D	E
1	-32				
2					
3					
4					

> **⚠ Caution**
>
> When working with Excel, it's better to enter the decimal equivalent instead of a fraction because Excel doesn't always interpret fractions as fractions. For example, Excel does interpret **1 3/4** as **1.75**. But if you enter just **3/4**, Excel thinks you've entered a date (March 4) and formats the entry as such. (You have to enter a **0** in front of the 3/4 for Excel to recognize it as a fraction.)

Entering Dates and Times

You might find it useful or necessary to incorporate date or time data into a spreadsheet. For example, you can enter sales data for specific dates or track web page clicks at specific times during the day. For this reason, Excel includes date and time formatting for its spreadsheets.

Dates can be expressed as *long dates* (Friday, August 22, 2014) or *short dates* (8/22/14). By default, time is expressed as hour:minute:second, followed by AM or PM, as follows: 8:23:00 PM.

To enter a date or time, move the cursor to the desired cell, using either your mouse or the arrow keys on your keyboard, and begin typing. The date or time you enter is echoed in the Formula bar. Press **Enter** when you're done.

To format your data as a date, enter numbers separated by the - or / characters. For example, you can enter either **2-14-82** or **2/14/82**. If you only enter the month and date (with no year), Excel changes the resulting date format to **14-Feb**. If you enter two digits for the year, as in **12/18/14**, Excel completes the year with the closest four digits. So if you enter **14** for the year, Excel makes it **2014**. If you enter **82**, Excel makes it **1982**.

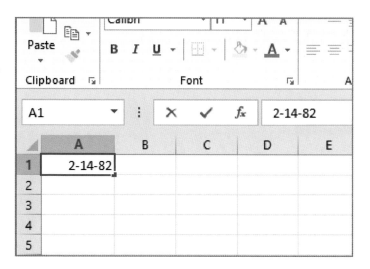

To format your data as time, enter numbers separated by the : character, followed by AM or PM. For example, to enter eleven fifty-five AM, enter **11:55 AM**. You can also enter seconds after the minute field, like this: **11:55:45 AM**. If you only enter hours (**9:**), Excel assumes zero minutes and zero seconds (9:00:00). If you enter only hours and minutes (**9:15**), Excel assumes zero seconds (9:15:00). If you don't specify AM or PM, Excel assumes AM.

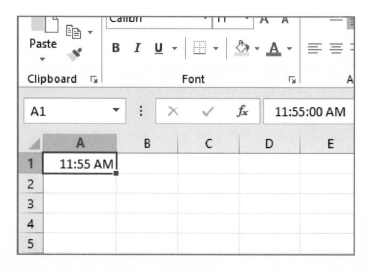

🕐 Tip

Excel includes additional formats for date and time, including many for other countries. Go to the **Number** section of the Home tab and click the **Expand** button to open the **Format Cells** dialog box. Click the **Number** tab and select a format **Category**. Many types of number formats have a Locale (location) control that enables you to select different countries.

Entering Text

	A	B	C	D	E	F		J
1		East	West	North	South			
2	Product A	200,000	150,000	250,000	180,000			
3	Product B	100,000	75,000	125,000	85,000			
4	Product C	500,000	600,000	750,000	400,000			
5	Product D	40,000	60,000	30,000	100,000			
6								
7								
8								
9								
10								
11								

Note

In Excel, the big difference between numbers and text is that you can't mathematically manipulate text. So you can format a number as "text" if you don't intend to use it in a calculation.

Most people think of Excel as an application for crunching numbers, but you also can use a spreadsheet to hold all manner of text-only data. As far as Excel is concerned, text isn't just the ABCs; data formatted as text can contain both alphabetic and numeric characters.

You could use text in a spreadsheet as a label for a row or column of numbers. You also can use text as raw data. For example, if you're cataloging the contents of your book collection, each cell can contain a book title in text format.

To enter text data, move the cursor to the desired cell, using either your mouse or the arrow keys on your keyboard, and begin typing. Press **Enter** when you're done.

Any data you enter that contains at least one alphabetic character (A, B, C, and so forth) is automatically formatted as text, even if it also contains numbers. So **Western Region**, for example, is automatically formatted as text, as is **7452 D**.

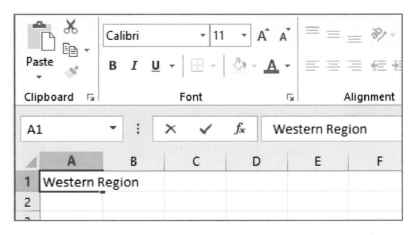

If you want to format a numeric entry as text, you have to do so manually; Excel doesn't recognize a cell containing all numbers as text. To apply text formatting to this type of data, be sure the **Home** tab is selected on the Ribbon, go to the **Number** section, pull down the **Number Format** list, and select **Text**.

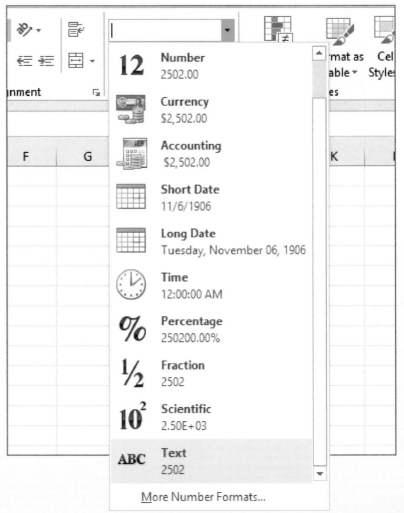

Editing Cell Data

Once you've entered data of any type into a spreadsheet, it's easy to edit that data, one cell at a time. You can make your edits directly within the active cell or use the Formula bar.

Do *not* simply move to a cell that already contains data and begin typing. Unless you press **F2** first (or double-click within the cell), any new data you enter will replace the existing data in the cell.

To edit data within the active cell, use your mouse or the arrow keys on your keyboard to move to the desired cell. Press the **F2** key to open the cell for editing, and move the cursor to the point within the cell where you want to make an edit. Use the **Delete** and **Backspace** keys to delete existing characters, and type the new information into the cell. Press **Enter** when you're done editing, and your changes are accepted into this cell.

To edit data in the Formula bar, use the mouse or arrow keys to move to the cell in question. Use your mouse to click in the **Formula** bar, and position the cursor at the point where you want to begin editing. Make the necessary changes, and press **Enter** (or click the ✓ icon next to the Formula bar) when you're done.

Tip

To accept changes to the current contents of the Formula bar, click the ✓ (Enter) icon to the left of the Formula bar. This has the same effect as pressing **Enter** on the keyboard. To reject changes, click the ✗ (Cancel) icon.

click to reject changes

click to accept changes

	A	B
1	2502	2500
2	2500	2200
3	2400	17

Deleting Data from a Cell

Sometimes you need to remove the data in a given cell or range of cells. You don't want to remove the cells themselves, which would then cause adjacent cells to move, but rather leave the cells empty.

By the way, deleting data is different from cutting it. When you cut data, it's copied to the Windows Clipboard, and you can paste it into another location. When you delete data, that data is gone. You can't paste it into another cell. You can, however, undo an accidental deletion. Press **Ctrl+Z** to undelete what you've just deleted.

1 Use your mouse or arrow keys to move to the cell that contains the data you want to delete.

2 Press the **Del** key on your keyboard. Alternatively, you can right-click the cell and select **Clear Contents** from the pop-up menu.

> 🕐 **Tip**
>
> To delete the contents of more than one cell at a time, press and hold the **Shift** key while selecting cells with your mouse or the arrow keys. This selects multiple cells, which you can delete with a single action. Do *not* right-click a cell and then click **Delete** from the pop-up menu. This removes the entire cell from the spreadsheet, not just the cell's contents. The surrounding cells then move up, down, or over to fill in the gap left by the deleted cell.

Finding and Replacing Text

With a small spreadsheet, it's easy enough to find a particular entry—just look for it on your screen. With larger spreadsheets, however, it becomes more difficult to find particular data points. Fortunately, Excel offers a robust search feature for spreadsheet data—and even lets you automatically replace selected bits of data.

1 To begin either the find or find-and-replace process, display the **Home** tab on the Ribbon, go to the **Editing** section, click the **Find & Select** button, and select either **Find…** or **Replace…** from the pull-down menu. This displays the Find and Replace dialog box. You can also display the Find and Replace dialog box by pressing the **Ctrl+F** keys on your keyboard.

> **Tip**
>
> If you know the location of a specific cell, you can go directly to it. Click the **Find & Select** button on the Ribbon, and select **Go To…**. When the Go To dialog box appears, enter the location (A1, B2, etc.) or the formal name of the given cell or range, and click **OK**.

2   To find a given number or phrase, click the **Find** tab and enter what you're looking for in the **Find what** box. To highlight all instances of this item, click the **Find All** button. To highlight only the first instance of this item, click the **Find Next** button. Then click **Find Next** again to display the next instance of this item, and again and again as necessary. Click **Close** when you're done.

3   To replace a given word or number with another word or number, click the **Replace** tab. Enter the text or number you want to replace in the **Find what** box, and enter the replacement text or number in the **Replace with** box. To globally replace all instances of this selection, click the **Replace All** button. To replace only the first instance of this item, click the **Replace** button. To replace the next instance of this item, click **Replace** again—and continue clicking **Replace** until you're done. Click **Close** when you're done.

If you're not sure how replacing a given selection will affect the contents of your spreadsheet, use the **Replace** button to make the changes one instance at a time. To undo a data replacement—that is, to revert to the original data—press **Ctrl+Z** on your keyboard.

Copying Cells

Sometimes you want to repeat data in another part of a spreadsheet. For example, you might want to use the same label for a row or column more than once. Or maybe you've created a formula (more on them later) and want to use that same formula on another selection of data.

When the need arises, it's often easier to copy an entire cell to another location than it is to re-enter the data by hand. When you copy cells this way, the content of the original cell remains intact, but it's also copied and pasted into the new location. If you paste into a cell with existing content, the copied content replaces the existing content.

> **Tip**
>
> You also can use keyboard shortcuts to copy and paste cells. Press **Ctrl+C** to copy a cell's contents, and press **Ctrl+V** to paste what you've copied.

1. Use your mouse or keyboard arrow keys to move to the cell you want to copy. Click the **Copy** button on the **Home** tab of the Ribbon.

2. Move to and select the new location for the cell data. Click the **Paste** button on the Home tab of the Ribbon.

Paste

Excel offers several different paste options when you're copying data from cell to cell. You access these options by clicking the down arrow on the **Paste** button on the Ribbon's **Home** tab. (More options are available when you select **Paste Special** to display the Paste Special dialog box.)

	Paste Option	Description
	Paste	This standard Paste command pastes the original content with its original formatting. It preserves any formulas from the original cell.
	Formulas	Pastes only the data and formulas from the original cell, not the formatting. The pasted data inherits the formatting of the target cell.
	Formulas & Number Formatting	Pastes the data and formulas. All numbers copied retain their original number formatting, but no other formatting is retained.
	Keep Source Formatting	Pastes the contents and the formatting of the original cells.
	No Borders	Pastes all the data, formulas, and formatting from the original cells except any borders from those cells.
	Keep Source Column Widths	Pastes data, formulas, and formatting from the original cell; also changes the column width of the new cell to match the width of the original.
	Transpose	Changes the orientation of the pasted entries. For example, if you copy a row of cells, it pastes them as a column.
	Values	Pastes only the calculated results of a formula, not the formula itself. Use this option to retain the calculated values and not apply the original formula to a new range of cells.
	Values & Number Formatting	Pastes the calculated results of a formula, along with all the formatting assigned to the original labels, values, and formulas in the source selection.
	Values & Source Formatting	Pastes the calculated results of a formula, along with all formatting assigned to the source cell range.
	Formatting	Pastes only the formatting, not the original cell's data. Use this option to apply one cell's formatting to another.
	Paste Link	When copying a formula, this retains the reference to the original source cells. (The formula doesn't change to reflect where it's been pasted to.)
	Picture	Pastes only pictures found in the original selection.
	Linked Picture	Pastes a link to the pictures in the original selection.

Moving Cells

Moving data is different from copying it. For starters, you use the Cut and Paste commands, not the Copy and Paste commands. When you cut a cell, it's no longer present in its original location; it only exists in the new location where you paste it. If you copy a cell, a copy remains in the original location. If you paste a cut cell into a cell with existing content, the pasted content replaces the existing content.

Note the Cut, Copy, and Paste commands only apply to the data and formatting within cells. If you want to insert a complete cell into a location in your spreadsheet (which then moves adjacent cells to make room for it), you use the Insert command.

1   Use the mouse or arrow keys to move to the cell you want to move. Click the **Cut** button on the **Home** tab of the Ribbon.

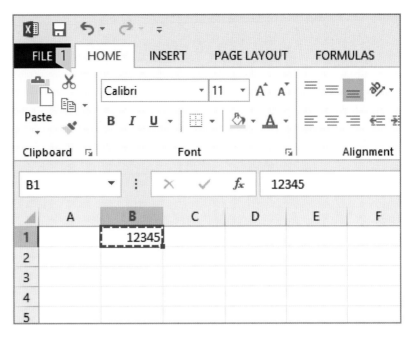

2   Move to and select the new location for the cell data. Click the **Paste** button on the **Home** tab of the Ribbon.

🕐 Tip

You also can use keyboard shortcuts to cut and paste cells. Press **Ctrl+X** to cut a cell's contents, and press **Ctrl+V** to paste those contents into another cell.

Chapter 3

Formatting Data

Plain letters and numbers in a grid may be practical, but they can have more impact when they're formatted in a useful and appealing fashion. It may help to bold column headings or put totals in a different color, for example. Or you might want to change the font or font size to make what's important larger.

Excel enables you to visually and practically format any piece of data you enter into a spreadsheet. You can change the font, size, color, and alignment of text and numbers. You also can apply different number formats, turning a simple string of numbers into currency, a fraction, a date, or scientific notation. You even can format a cell's background shading and borders.

Most Excel formatting is done via the Ribbon's Home tab. In most instances, formatting the contents of a cell is as easy as clicking a button on the Ribbon.

In This Chapter

- Formatting with bold, italic, and other font effects
- Wrapping and aligning text
- Centering multiple-column text
- Formatting cell background color
- Formatting numbers and currency
- Formatting cells conditionally
- Formatting tables
- Working with borders
- Copying formatting from one cell to another

Applying Bold, Italic, and Other Font Effects

You can format text and numbers within a cell with various font effects—bold, italic, underline, double underline, and color. You can apply these font effects to the entire contents of a cell or just to selected characters within the cell.

Font effects help you highlight cells or individual words or numbers that are more important or need special emphasis. Use font effects in a spreadsheet the same way you would in a written document—sparingly, and only to draw attention to specific contents. It's okay to format labels and totals differently from surrounding data, but you don't want to format each column of data in a spreadsheet a different color, for example.

To format the entire contents of a cell, use your keyboard or mouse to select that cell. You also can select multiple cells to format them all at once with the same effects.

To format selected words or characters in an individual cell, start by selecting that cell. Move to the Formula bar, and use your mouse to highlight the characters you want to format.

> **Tip**
>
> To clear all formatting from a cell, including font and number formatting, select the cell, click the **Clear** button in the Editing section of the Home tab on the Ribbon, and select **Clear Formats**. You can use the other options on the Clear button to clear everything from a cell (Clear All), clear only the contents and retain the formatting, clear comments, or clear hyperlinks.

With the cell or individual characters highlighted, move to the **Font** section of the **Home** tab and click the effect you want to apply. Click **Bold** (or press **Ctrl+B**) to bold the selection. Click **Italic** (or press **Ctrl+I**) to italicize the selection. Click **Underline** (or press **Ctrl+U**) to underline the selection. Click the down-arrow on the **Underline** button and select **Double Underline** to apply a double underline effect.

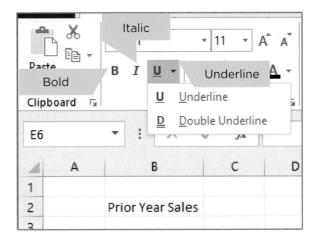

To change font color, click the down-arrow next to the **Font Color** button on the **Home** tab. Select **Automatic** to apply Excel's automatic formatting for this type of content (typically black), select one of the Theme Colors to apply a color from the selected theme, or select one of the Standard Colors to apply one of the standard system colors.

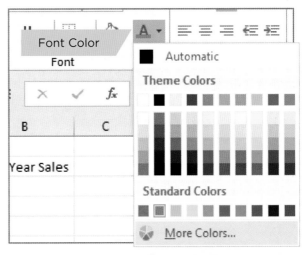

To apply a custom color, click the down-arrow next to the **Font Color** button and select **More Colors** to open the **Colors** dialog box. Click either the **Standard** or **Custom** tabs to view available selections, and click the color you want. (The Custom tab lets you select specific red, green, and blue color values.) Click **OK** to apply the selected color.

The last color you selected is displayed on the Font Color button. To apply this color to a new selection, just click the **Font Color** button.

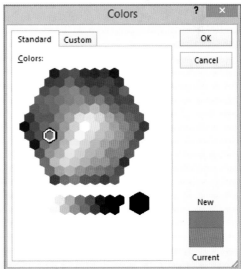

Changing Font and Font Size

Just as you can change the look of a cell or selected contents by applying bold, italic, and other font effects, you can also change a selection's font and font size. This is particularly useful when formatting labels, headings, and the like that need to stand out from the surrounding cells.

Changing the font for a range of cells can change the feel of a spreadsheet and even improve a spreadsheet's readability. For example, cell contents formatted with the Times Roman font look a little fancier than those formatted with the Ariel or Verdana fonts, which look a little cleaner and can be easier to read, especially for numbers. And you'll appreciate the ability to make less-important numbers smaller while enlarging more-important numbers for improved readability.

To format the entire contents of a cell, use your keyboard or mouse to select that cell. You also can select multiple cells to format them all at once with the same effects.

To format selected words or characters in an individual cell, start by selecting that cell. Move to the Formula bar, and use your mouse to highlight the characters you want to format.

To apply a different font, go to the **Font** section of the **Home** tab, click the down-arrow next to the **Font** list, and make a selection.

To change the size of the font, click the down-arrow next to the **Font Size** list and make a selection. Alternatively, click the **Increase Font Size** or **Decrease Font Size** buttons to increase or decrease the size of the font.

You can also change font, font size, and other attributes from the Format Cells dialog box. Display this dialog box by clicking the **Expand** button at the lower-right corner of the **Font** section of the **Home** tab and then select the **Font** tab. You can now change Font, Font Style, Size, Underline style, Color, and other Effects, and see a preview of your changes. Click **OK** when you're done.

✎ Note

Excel's default font is Calibri, size 11 points.

Aligning Text

By default, any text you enter into a cell is aligned to the left. Numbers are aligned to the right, but you can change the horizontal alignment of any cell. Excel lets you align a cell's content left, right, or centered—although you'll probably want to keep all your numbers right aligned for better readability.

Select the cell or cells you want to align, and go to the **Alignment** section of the **Home** tab. Click **Align Left**, **Center**, or **Align Right**.

For further horizontal alignment options, click the **Expand** button at the lower-right corner of the **Alignment** section to open the Format Cells dialog box. Select the **Alignment** tab, pull down the **Horizontal** list, and make a new selection. This list offers several options: General (aligns text left and numbers right), Left (indent), Center, Right (indent), Fill, Justify, Center Across Selection, and Distributed (indent). For Left, Right, and Distributed alignment, you can use the Indent list to indent the text from the edge of the cell. Click **OK** to apply the new alignment.

Aligning Text Vertically

In addition to aligning text or numbers horizontally within a cell (left, right, or centered), you can vertically align cell contents. You can have cell contents align to the top of the cell, the bottom of the cell, or vertically centered within the cell.

Vertical alignment is necessary when some cells in a row are filled with more data than other cells in the same row. Imagine a single cell containing a large block of text and the next cell to the left or right containing a single short number. The height of all cells in the row are the same, so where do you want that lonely little number to appear—at the top, at the bottom, or in the middle of the cell?

By default, data is vertically aligned to the bottom of a cell.

Select the cell or cells you want to align, and go to the **Alignment** section of the **Home** tab and click either **Top Align**, **Middle Align**, or **Bottom Align**.

For further vertical alignment options, click the **Expand** button at the lower-right corner of the **Alignment** section to open the Format Cells dialog box. Select the **Alignment** tab, pull down the **Vertical** list, and make a new selection. This list offers Top, Center, Bottom, Justify, and Distributed alignment. Click **OK** to apply the new alignment.

Note

In most instances, Justify and Distributed have the same effect—adding space between each line so the text is spread evenly top to bottom within the cell. These options have different effects on vertically flowing text, such as you have with some Asian languages.

Wrapping Text Within a Cell

If you have a lot of text in a single cell, it might overflow the column boundaries. In this case, you can make the column wider or format the contents to better fit within the cell.

The best approach is to make long text wrap within the cell. That means the text is automatically formatted with line breaks so the text wraps downward instead of running past the right edge of the cell. When you choose to wrap text within a cell, the height of that cell (and the entire row of cells) is automatically expanded so all the text is visible.

1 Select the cell with the long text.

2 Click the **Wrap Text** button in the **Alignment** section of the **Home** tab of the Ribbon. You can then choose to left align, right align, center, or justify the text horizontally within the cell.

Centering Text Across Multiple Columns

If your page or table has a title or header, you could center that title across more than one column of data. To do this, you must first merge the affected cells into a single cell and then center align the data within that merged cell. You can merge cells across multiple columns as well as cells that span more than one row. You even can merge cells that span multiple rows and columns. Excel always retains the contents of the left- or top-left-most cell in the selected range. All contents of other merged cells are deleted, so be sure to account for this before you merge any cells.

Tip

Click the down-arrow next to the **Merge & Center** button for more options: Merge Across (merges cells within a single row, even if multiple rows are selected), Merge Cells (merges cells and applies general alignment instead of centering), or Unmerge Cells.

1 Enter the appropriate text into the left-most cell of the selected area.

2 Select all the cells across which you want to center the text.

3 Click the **Merge & Center** button in the **Alignment** section of the **Home** tab.

Rotating Text

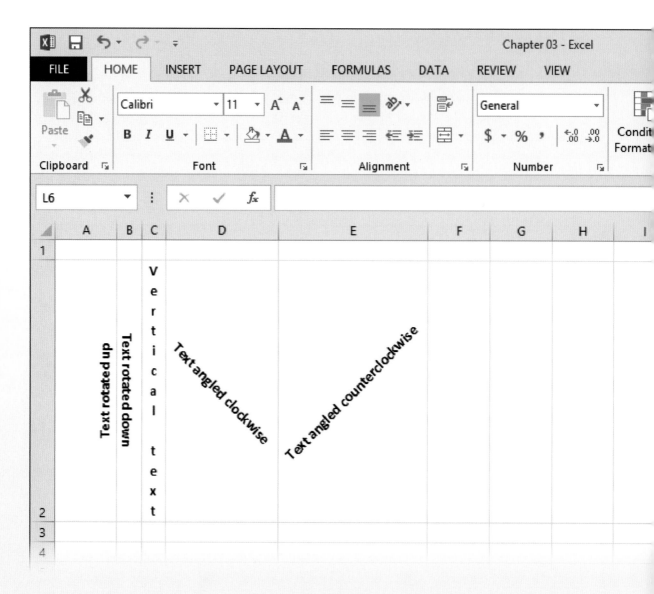

A spreadsheet's text doesn't always have to run horizontally, left to right. When you're formatting tables and other visually sophisticated representations of your data, you can run some of your text vertically, from the bottom of a cell up to the top. Excel also enables you to rotate text to any degree so you can have text running diagonally across a cell.

1 Select the cell that contains the text you want to rotate, and click the down-arrow next to the **Orientation** button in the **Alignment** section of the **Home** tab on the Ribbon. From the menu of options, select the type of rotation you want. You can choose from Angle Counterclockwise, Angle Clockwise, Vertical Text, Rotate Text Up, or Rotate Text Down.

2 To apply a custom degree of rotation, click the down-arrow next to the **Orientation** button and then select **Format Cell Alignment** to display the Format Cells dialog box. Select the **Alignment** tab and then use the **Degrees** control in the Orientation section to specify the precise degree of rotation. (You can also enter the degree of rotation into the Degrees box.) Click **OK** to apply the rotation effect.

> **Note**
>
> Don't confuse text rotated 90 degrees with what Excel calls *vertical text*. A 90-degree rotation reads normally when you turn your head to the side. Vertical text, on the other hand, doesn't rotate the characters, but rather spells the words one character at a time running from top to bottom in the cell.

Applying a Background Color

In addition to changing the color of text and numbers in a cell, you can change the color of the cell itself by applying a specific background color to the cell.

Applying cell background colors is useful when formatting specific types of data in a spreadsheet. For example, you can change the background color for those cells used as row or column headers or for the title of a table. You also might want to choose a different background color for different types of data, such as column or row totals. Different colors are also helpful when you want to highlight the data in specific cells in a spreadsheet.

1 Select the cell or cells whose background color you want to change.

2 Click the **Fill Color** button to apply the currently selected background color.

3 Click the down-arrow next to the **Fill Color** button to display Theme Colors and Standard Colors. Click a color to apply it to the selected cells, or click **No Fill** to remove any background color from the cells.

4 To choose from additional colors, click **More Colors...** to display the Colors dialog box.

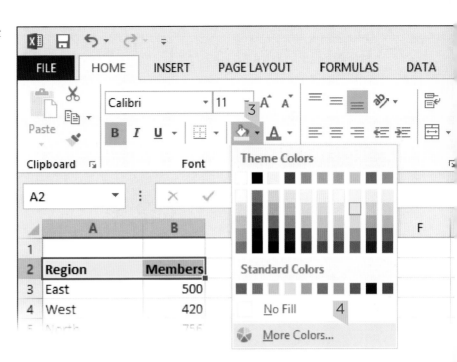

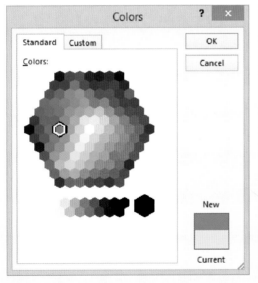

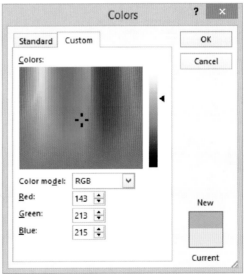

5 Click the **Standard** tab to select from the full array of standard system colors. Click a color to select it, and click **OK**.

6 Click the **Custom** tab to apply a custom color to the selected cells. You can click anywhere on the color selector or specify exact Red, Green, and Blue color values. Click **OK** to apply the selected color.

Applying Number Formats

	Number Format	Example
1	**Number Format**	**Example**
2	General	325400
3	Number	325400.00
4	Comma	325,400
5	Currency (U.S. dollars)	$325.07
6	Currency (Euros)	€ 325.50
7	Accounting (U.S. dollars)	$ 325.07
8	Short date	2/14/2014
9	Long date	Friday, February 14, 2014
10	Time	11:30:00 AM
11	Percentage	45%
12	Fraction	1/4
13	Scientific notation	2.50E+05

Numbers are the heart and soul of a spreadsheet. But there are many kinds of numbers—simple numbers with no commas, numbers with comma separators every 3 digits, percentages, fractions, numbers expressed in scientific notation, currency (in a variety of national formats—dollars, pounds, Euros, and the like), and even times and dates expressed numerically.

When you enter a number into a cell, by default Excel applies a general number format—straight numbers, with no commas or decimal points. If you want to express a number differently, you need to apply a specific number format.

1 Select the cell or cells you want to format, and click one of the buttons in the **Number** section of the **Home** tab on the Ribbon. You can choose from Accounting Number Format, Percent Style, or Comma Style.

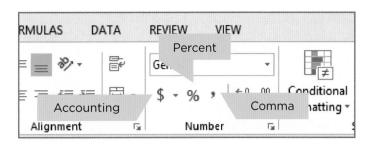

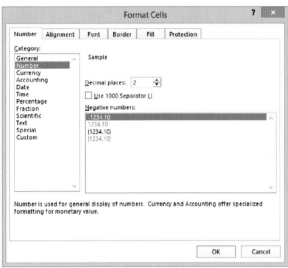

2 Additional number formats are available from the Number Format list in the **Number** section. Select the format you want from this list.

3 To view all available number formats, click the **Expand** button at the lower-right corner of the **Number** section. This displays the Format Cells dialog box. Click the **Number** tab, and select a type of number format from the **Category** list. Within the selected category, customize the available options. For example, if you select the **Number** category, you can specify how many decimal places to display and whether or not to display the comma separator. Click **OK** to apply the selected format.

Changing Currency Formats

Excel is a program designed to be used across national boundaries in our global economy. As such, you can choose to display numbers in a variety of national currency formats, from Armenian to Zimbabwean. You're not limited to American dollars and cents.

Select the cell or cells you want to format, and click the down-arrow next to the **Accounting Number Format** button on the **Home** tab of the Ribbon. Choose from the currencies listed there—United States dollars, British pounds, Euros, Chinese yuan, or French francs.

To choose from additional currencies, click the down-arrow next to the **Accounting Number Format** button and select **More Accounting Formats…**. Select **Accounting** or **Currency** in the **Category** list. Then pull down the **Symbol** list, and select the desired currency. Click **OK** when you're done.

> ✏ **Note**
>
> The Accounting Number and Currency formats are similar in that they both use the appropriate currency symbols with the numbers. The Accounting Number format aligns both the currency symbols and the decimal points in columns, which then aligns the currency symbol to the left. The Currency format keeps the currency symbol next to the number itself and aligns everything to the right.

Displaying Decimal Places

In Excel's default general number format, no decimal places are displayed; you must enter them manually. For example, if you enter **123**, Excel displays **123**; if you enter **123.4**, Excel displays **123.4**.

Other number formats, such as the Currency format, automatically add the appropriate number of decimal places. (That's two places, in the case of the Currency format.) You can, however, manually select how many decimal places to display for the number in a given cell.

To add digits after the decimal point, select the cell or cells you want to format, and click the **Increase Decimal** button in the **Number** section of the **Home** tab on the Ribbon. Click the **Decrease Decimal** button to remove digits after the decimal point. For example, if you enter **123** and click the **Increase Decimal** button one time, the number is expressed as **123.0**. If you enter **123.44** and click the **Decrease Decimal** button, the number is rounded down and expressed as **123.4**.

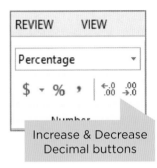

Increase & Decrease Decimal buttons

You can also select how many decimal places to display from the Format Cell dialog box. Select the cell or cells and click the **Expand** button in the lower-right corner of the **Number** section of the **Home** tab on the Ribbon. When the Format Cells dialog box appears, select the **Number** tab and the **Category** you want. Most categories have a Decimal places control; use the up and down arrows to select the number of decimal places to display, or just enter the number in the **Decimal places** box. Click **OK** when you're done.

Using Automatic Number Formats

It's easy enough to apply Excel's number formats to cells that already contain data, but it's even easier to have Excel automatically format your numbers as you enter them. Depending on how you enter a number, Excel can automatically apply a specific format to that number. Notice that as you enter numbers into a cell, Excel updates the Number Format area when it recognizes what you're entering.

To enter a decimal number, enter the decimal point as part of the number, like this: **123.45** (including the decimal point).

To enter currency, enter the dollar sign (**$**) before entering the numerical value, like this: **$35**. You also can enter decimal values, like this: **$29.95**.

> **Tip**
>
> To automatically format a number as a time, include a colon (**:**) between the hours, minutes, or seconds, like this: **10:45**. Entering an **A** or **P** after a number (like this: **10 A**) also formats it as a time. To automatically format scientific notation, enter an **E** (uppercase or lowercase) before the exponential term, like this: **10e4**.

To enter a percentage, enter the numerical value followed by the percent sign (%), like this: **50%**. Or enter decimal values, like this: **40.5%**.

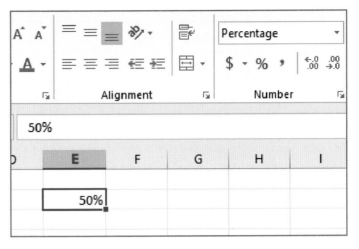

To enter a fraction, enter the following in order: **0** (zero), **space**, **numerator** (top number), **slash** (/), and **denominator**. For example, to display the fraction 1/4, enter this: **0 1/4**.

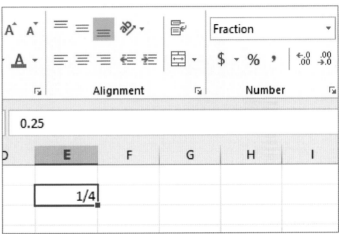

To enter a date, enter the month, a dash or slash, and the day. For example, entering **1-12** or **1/12** displays as **12-Jan**. You can also enter the year—preceded by a hyphen or slash. For example, if you enter **1-12-15**, Excel displays **1/12/2015**.

Using Conditional Formatting

For certain types of data, you might want to express different values in different colors, or with different accompanying symbols. This helps readers visually grasp the different values in the spreadsheet.

For example, if you're displaying a range of temperatures for various locations over time, you can shade the cells so the highest temperatures are a different color than the lowest temperatures. If you have a table that details grade point averages for a group of students over several semesters, you can assign green checkmarks to the highest grades and red X's to the lowest ones.

This is called conditional formatting, and Excel offers a variety of different formats and approaches to apply conditional formatting to your data.

Select the range of values you want conditionally formatted, and click the **Conditional Formatting** button in the **Styles** section of the **Home** tab. To conditionally format cells that are less than or greater than a given value, or contain specific text, or contain a specific date, click **Highlight Cells Rules** and select a type of rule. When prompted, enter the values you want highlighted as well as the formatting effect.

To highlight the top and bottom data in the selection (by rank, percentage, or above/below average), click **Top/Bottom Rules** and then select a type of rule. When prompted, select the desired formatting effect.

To display colored data bars inside each cell, corresponding to the cell's value, click **Data Bars** and select a type of gradient or solid fill.

Region	Members
East	500
West	420
North	756
South	500

To display cells in a range of colors corresponding to data values, click **Color Scales** and select a color scheme.

Region	Members
East	500
West	420
North	756
South	500

To display icons such as colored check marks or arrows in the cells that correspond to the data values, click **Icon Sets** and select the desired icons or shapes.

Region	Members
East	500
West	420
North	756
South	500

◑ Tip

To create custom conditional formatting, click the **Conditional Formatting** button and select **New Rule**. This displays the New Formatting Rule dialog box. Select a rule type, edit the rule description, and click **OK** to apply the rule to the selected cells.

Using Conditional Formatting

Applying Cell Styles

Excel includes a variety of built-in cell styles you can apply to any cell or cells with a click of the mouse. These cell styles apply a specific font, font size, font color, and cell color to selected cells.

Excel includes cell styles for Good, Bad, and Neutral data; explanatory text, notes, linked cells, and the like; titles and headings; popular number formats; and basic color schemes.

1   Select the cell or cells you want to format.

2   Click the **Cell Styles** button in the **Styles** section of the **Home** tab on the Ribbon, and click the style you want to apply.

Creating a New Cell Style

If you tend to use a specific type of formatting over and over in your spreadsheets, you might want to add it to Excel's built-in cell styles. Then you can apply your personal formatting with a single click, rather than going through a complex multistep formatting process.

The easiest way to create a new cell style is by example. That is, format a sample cell to your liking, and use that cell to create the new cell style.

1 Format a cell using your preferred font, font size, font color, and background color. You also can include number formatting and borders. Select that cell, click the **Cell Styles** button, and click **New Cell Style…**.

2 When the Style dialog box appears, enter a name for this new cell style in the **Style name** box. Uncheck any item you don't want included in the style. By default, the cell style includes number format, alignment, font (type, size, and color), border, fill, and protection (locked or unlocked). Click **OK** to add the style to Excel's cell style list.

Adding Borders

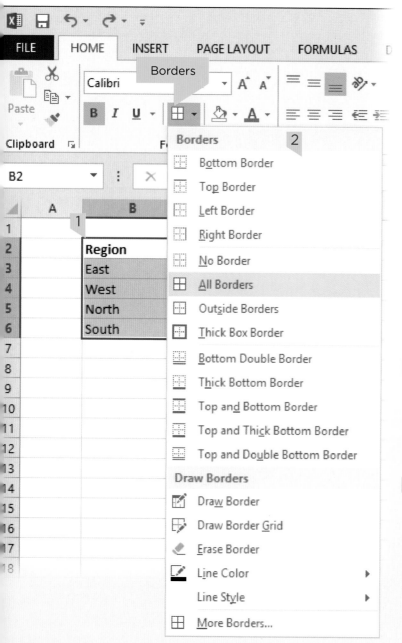

One way to focus attention on a particular selection of data is to surround that selection with a border. In Excel, you can draw a border completely around a cell or group of cells or apply it to one or more sides of the selection. This last feature lets you place a border above or below (or both) a row of totals, for example. You can even draw borders around the individual cells within a larger range.

When you're adding borders to a selection, you can choose the line style (solid or dashed), weight (thin or thick), and color. You can use Excel's built-in border styles or customize the borders for a selected range of cells as you like.

1 Select the cell or range of cells you want to border, and click the down-arrow next to the **Borders** button in the **Font** section of the **Home** tab on the Ribbon.

2 Select the border parts and styles you want to apply to this section. You can choose to draw top, bottom, left, and right borders; outside borders only or "all borders" around each cell in the selection; and various combinations of top and bottom borders only. To remove all borders from a selection, click the **Borders** down-arrow and select **No Border**.

1. To customize the borders for a selected cell or range of cells, click the down-arrow next to the **Borders** button and select **More Borders...**. This displays the Format Cells dialog box; select the **Border** tab.

2. Select a line style for this border from the **Style** list, and select a color from the **Color** list.

3. To apply the border around the selected range of cells, click **Outline** in the **Presets** section. To apply a border to all the cells inside the selected range, click **Inside**.

4. To apply the border to a specific side of selected cells, click the appropriate location button in the **Border** section. You'll see how the border looks in the preview located in the middle of the dialog box. If you decide not to add a particular border, simply unclick its button in the Border section. Click **OK** when you're done.

> **Tip**
>
> You also can manually draw borders around cells in your spreadsheet. To do this, click the **Borders** down-arrow, go to the **Draw Border** section of the menu, and select a line color and style. Click **Draw Border**, and move to the spreadsheet and use your mouse to draw the border wherever you want it.

Copying Cell Formatting

After you've formatted a cell the way you like, you might find that you want to apply that same format to other selections in your spreadsheet. You could manually format those other cells the same way, but that takes a lot of time and effort. It's a lot easier to simply copy the formatting from a given cell to another cell or group of cells in the spreadsheet.

The easiest way to copy cell formatting is with Excel's Format Painter tool. This tool copies all cell formatting—font, font size, font color, cell color, borders, even number formats—with a few clicks of the mouse. You can even copy a single cell's format to multiple locations within your spreadsheet.

Note the Format Painter tool only copies cell formatting, not the contents of the original cell. So you can apply formatting to another cell that already contains data without fear of losing the data in the destination cell.

1 Format a cell the way you like, or choose a cell that's formatted in the proper fashion. Select that cell.

2 Click the **Format Painter** button in the **Clipboard** section of the **Home** tab on the Ribbon.

3 To copy the formatting to a single cell, click the destination cell. To copy the formatting to a range of cells, drag the mouse across the range of cells. The original cell's formatting is now applied to the new selection.

> **Tip**
>
> To copy formatting to several nonadjacent cells, or to multiple nonadjacent ranges, select the original cell and *double-click* the **Format Painter** button. Click or drag across each new selection in turn to apply the formatting. When you're done, either click the **Format Painter** button again or press the **Esc** key to turn off the tool.

Chapter 4

Working with Rows and Columns

A spreadsheet is nothing more than a big grid of rows and columns. Rows run horizontally (side by side) while columns run vertically (up and down). Where a given row and column intersect you have a single cell.

Much of the data you enter into a spreadsheet is arranged in either rows or columns. For example, if you're listing your income by year, each year's income data might be listed in the same column, with a different row for each year. If you're listing invoices by number, all the invoice numbers might appear in the same column.

Likewise, if you're creating a chore chart for the members of your family, all your family members might be listed in the same row, each with his or her own column. If you're tracking hours worked per day, you might list the days in a single row across the top of the data.

Given Excel's dependence on the row-and-column grid, you'll be working with rows and columns a lot, moving them around, inserting new ones, deleting unused ones, and the like. In this chapter, you learn what you can do with Excel's rows and columns and how to do it all.

In This Chapter

- Assigning names to rows, columns, and cells
- Setting column width and row height
- Inserting and deleting rows and columns
- Inserting and deleting single cells
- Copying and moving rows and columns
- Hiding and unhiding rows and columns
- Locking a row or column in place
- Merging and splitting cells
- Sorting data by column

Understanding Rows and Columns

The spreadsheet grid is composed of a seemingly endless series of rows and columns. Excel labels its columns alphabetically (A, B, C, and so on) from left to right. Rows are labeled numerically (1, 2, 3, and so on) from top to bottom. The point where each column and row intersect is an individual cell. Each cell is referenced by its location—that is, the intersection of column and row. For example, the very top left cell—in the first column (A), in the first row (1)—is labeled A1. The cell located in the second column (B), second row (2) position is labeled B2. Each cell's unique location is called the cell reference, which is always expressed as column first, row second. (You can view the cell reference in Excel's Name Box, right beside the formula bar above the spreadsheet itself.)

When you first create a spreadsheet, all the rows are the same height and all the columns are the same width. This works fine until you start entering data. If you enter a long string of text into a cell, it stretches beyond the column boundary. If you wrap that text within the cell, it's taller than the default row height. Fortunately, Excel lets you resize entire rows and columns. In fact, each column or row can be sized differently, if need be.

To select an entire row—that is, to select all the cells in a particular row—click the row header. For example, to select all the cells in the second row, click the **2** to the left of that row. To deselect a row, click anywhere else in the spreadsheet.

Similarly, you can select an entire column by clicking the column header. For example, to select all the cells in the second column, click the **B** at the top of that column. Click anywhere else in the spreadsheet to deselect that column.

When you select an entire row or column, you can then make changes to all the cells in that row or column at one time. For example, you can select a row and then format that row's font, font size, font color, cell background color—you name it. You also can copy, move, or delete entire rows and columns you've selected. In essence, when you select a row or column, Excel treats all the cells in that row or column as a single item.

Naming Cells, Rows, and Columns

When you want to reference the contents of a given cell, you do so by its location. For example, if you want to reference the first cell in the first column of a worksheet, you call it cell A1. (Remember, spreadsheet columns are identified by letter, rows are identified by number, and each individual cell is identified by its column-and-row position. So the cell in the second column of the second row is B2.)

This location-based nomenclature works fine until you move a cell, or the cell shifts because you insert a new column or row in front of it. When that happens, the cell's location changes. Unfortunately, any formulas you've created still reference the original location, not the changed one.

The solution is to assign a unique name to that cell that follows the cell even if its location changes. You can also assign names to entire rows and columns for the same purpose. Naming a cell, row, or column also has the advantage of being easier to remember than the location reference. So for example, if you've named cells A1 and A2 as New and Old, respectively, you can add them together using this formula: **=New+Old**. You could also sum the contents of a column named Budget like this: **=sum(Budget)**.

1. Select the cell, row, or column you want to name.

2. Select the **Formulas** tab on the Ribbon, go to the **Defined Names** section, and click the **Define Name** button.

3. When the New Name dialog box appears, enter a name for the selected cell, row, or column in the **Name** box. Click **OK** to apply that name to the selected cell, row, or column.

Note

The assigned name of a cell, row, or column is shown in the Name Box when that item is selected in the spreadsheet.

Naming Cells, Rows, and Columns   77

Changing Column Width

If the data you enter into a cell is too long, you'll only see the first part of that data—there'll be a bit to the right that looks cut off. It's not really cut off; it just can't be seen because the text or number is longer than the width of the current column.

You can fix this problem by adjusting the column width. Wider columns allow you to see more data, whereas narrow columns let you display more columns per page.

1 Move the cursor to the column header, and position it on the dividing line on the right side of the column you want to adjust.

2 When the cursor changes shape, click your mouse's left button and drag the column divider to the right (to make a wider column) or to the left (to make a smaller column). Release the mouse button when the column is the width you want it.

Changing Row Height

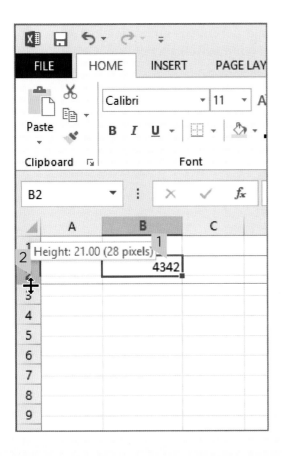

If you change the font size of text in a given row, Excel automatically adjusts the row height to match. The same is true if you wrap long spans of text. However, you might still want to change a row's height. The operation is similar to changing a column's width.

1 Move the cursor to the row header to the left of the row you want to adjust, and position it on the line on the bottom border of that row.

2 When the cursor changes shape, hold down the left mouse button and drag the row divider down (to make a taller row) or up (to make a shorter row). Release the mouse button when the row is the height you want it.

🕐 Tip

To apply a more precise row height, select the row and go to the **Cells** section of the **Home** tab on the Ribbon. Click **Format**, **Row Height**, and when the Row Height dialog box appears, enter the exact height into the **Row Height** box. Click **OK** to apply the new height. You can adjust column width similarly. Choose **Column Width** instead of Row Height in the **Format** section, and adjust as you like. To make a row the exact height for the largest text or number entered, position your cursor over the dividing line on the bottom of the row header and double-click your mouse. This makes the row height automatically "fit" your current data.

Inserting a New Row

There will be times when you'll need to return to an existing spreadsheet and insert new information. Often you'll need to insert entire new rows for the additional data. When you insert a new row into your spreadsheet, all the existing rows after the new one are moved down accordingly. No data is deleted; everything just moves down one.

new row is inserted before selected row

1 Click the row header *after* where you want to make the insertion. You insert the new row *before* the selected row.

2 Go to the **Cells** section of the **Home** tab on the Ribbon, and click the **Insert** button. A new empty row is inserted, and all rows after this one are shifted down.

Inserting a New Column

Inserting a new column into a spreadsheet is similar to inserting a new row. When you insert a new column, all existing columns after the new are moved to the right. No data is deleted.

new column is inserted
before selected column

1 Click the column header *after* where you want to make the insertion. You insert the new column *before* the selected column.

2 Go to the **Cells** section of the **Home** tab on the Ribbon, and click the **Insert** button. A new empty column is inserted, and all columns after this one are shifted to the right.

Deleting a Row

Sometimes you might not organize data in the most efficient fashion, especially when you're creating a spreadsheet bit by bit. If you end up with an empty row you don't need, you can delete that row to make better use of your screen real estate. When you delete an entire row, all the subsequent rows are shifted up to fill the empty space.

1 Click the header for the row you want to delete.

2 Go to the **Cells** section of the **Home** tab on the Ribbon, and click the **Delete** button. The selected row is deleted, and all the rows after that one are moved up to fill the space.

> **! Caution**
>
> Excel lets you delete rows and columns that contain data you no longer use. Just know that when you delete a row or column, all the data and formulas in those cells are deleted as well. If a deleted row or column contains cells referenced elsewhere in a formula, that formula will be affected.

Deleting a Column

Just as you can delete entire rows of a spreadsheet, you can also delete entire columns. When you delete a column, all remaining columns to the right of the deleted one are shifted to the left.

1 Click the header for the column you want to delete.

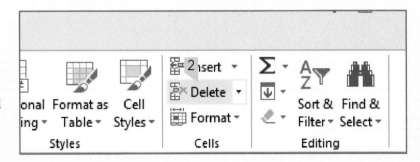

2 Go to the **Cells** section of the **Home** tab on the Ribbon, and click the **Delete** button. The selected column is deleted, and all the columns beyond that one are moved left to fill the space.

Inserting a Single Cell

Inserting a new cell into a spreadsheet isn't as straightforward as inserting an entire row or column. The existing cells have to shift to make room for the new cell—but do they shift down or to the right?

That's a decision you have to make when you choose to insert a cell. There's no universal way to approach this. You have to make the decision based on the data in a given spreadsheet.

> **Tip**
>
> To insert more than one adjacent cell into your spreadsheet, select multiple cells instead of just a single cell.

| 1 | Use your mouse or your keyboard arrow keys to move to the place in the spreadsheet where you want to insert a new cell. |

| 2 | Go to the **Cells** section of the Home tab on the Ribbon, click the right-arrow next to the **Insert** button, and click **Insert Cells…**. |

| 3 | When the Insert dialog box appears, select how you want the existing cells to shift. You can choose to **Shift cells right** or **Shift cells down**. (You can also opt to shift the entire row or column if you want.) Click **OK** when you're done, and a new empty cell will be inserted at the current position. |

Deleting a Single Cell

Deleting an entire cell is different from deleting the *contents* of a cell. When you remove a cell's contents, the cell framework remains; you're left with an empty cell. When you delete the entire cell, however, the cell is removed completely, data and all. This leaves you with a hole in your spreadsheet, and Excel will need to move adjacent cells to fill that hole.

After you delete a cell, you can choose to shift cells beneath it up or shift cells beside it to the left. You can also choose to delete the entire row or column instead of a single cell. This option is useful if you're deleting a cell in an otherwise empty row or column.

One word of caution: deleting a cell can wreak havoc on the formatting of a spreadsheet, as well as the construction of formulas that reference the deleted cell. At times, you might be better off deleting just the data within the cell rather than the cell itself.

1 Use your mouse or your keyboard arrow keys to move to the cell you want to delete.

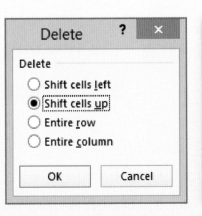

2 Go to the **Cells** section of the **Home** tab on the Ribbon, click the right-arrow next to the **Delete** button, and click **Delete Cells…**.

3 When the Delete dialog box appears, select which cells you want to move to fill in the space left by the deleted cell. You can choose to **Shift cells left** (from the right) or **Shift cells up** (from below). You can also opt to delete the entire row or column if you want. Click **OK** when you're done, and the designated cells will be moved into place.

Tip

To delete more than one adjacent cell at a time, hold **Shift** while selecting cells with your mouse. To select more than one nonadjacent cells, press and hold **Ctrl** while clicking each cell.

Copying a Row or Column

Excel enables you to copy an entire row or column to a new location within a spreadsheet. When you copy a row or column, the original data remains in its original location and also appears in its new location. This is different from moving data. When you move a row or column, the original data no longer exists in the original location.

Replacing Data

There are two ways to copy rows and columns. With this first approach, you paste the copied data over any existing data, formulas, or formatting in the destination location.

1 Click the row or column header for the row or column you want to copy. Go to the **Clipboard** section of the **Home** tab on the Ribbon, and click the **Copy** button.

2 Click the row or column header for the destination location, go to the **Clipboard** section of the **Home** tab on the Ribbon, and click the **Paste** button. The contents of the original row or column are now pasted into the destination location— and still remain in their original location as well.

original column

destination column

	A	B	C	D	E	F
1		Region	Members	Donations	Pledged	
2		North	42	$ 500.00	$ 500.00	
3		South	32	$ 425.00	$ 400.00	
4		East	38	$ 450.00	$ 480.00	
5		West	41	$ 480.00	$ 500.00	

⚠ Caution

Using this approach to copy a row or column to another position completely deletes all the contents of the original destination row or column, including all data, formulas, and formatting.

Inserting Data

When you copy and *replace* a row or column, all the data in the original destination row or column is overwritten. If there's no data in the destination row or column, this isn't a problem. If, on the other hand, you want to keep the existing data in the destination location, you need to *insert* a new row or column in which to paste the row or column you've copied. This approach moves all subsequent rows or columns to make room for the copied data.

1 Click the row or column header for the row or column you want to copy. Go to the **Clipboard** section of the **Home** tab on the Ribbon, and click the **Copy** button.

	A	B	C	D	E	F
1		Region	Members	Donations	Pledged	
2		North	42	$ 500.00	$ 500.00	
3		South	32	$ 425.00	$ 400.00	
4		East	38	$ 450.00	$ 480.00	
5		West	41	$ 480.00	$ 500.00	
6						
7						
8						
9						

2 Click the row or column header for the destination data, go to the **Cells** section of the **Home** tab on the Ribbon, click the **Insert** button, and click **Insert Copied Cells**. This inserts a new row or column at the selected location and pastes the copied data into this location.

Moving a Row or Column

Sometimes you need to rearrange the data you've entered into a spreadsheet. Maybe you put lodging in front of dining in an expense report, and your boss wants it the other way around. Maybe you accidentally entered an entire column of 2014 expenses before the 2013 column and need to switch them. Maybe you don't like things where they are and want to move them around a bit.

Excel lets you easily move a row or column from one position to another in the spreadsheet grid. When you move a row or column, it literally moves; there's no original data left in its original location, as there is when you use the copy function.

Replacing Data

There are two ways to move rows and columns. This first approach replaces the destination row location with the moved data. Note that using this method means you lose all existing data, formulas, and formatting in the destination location.

1 Click the row or column header for the row or column you want to move. Go to the **Clipboard** section of the **Home** tab on the Ribbon, and click the **Cut** button.

2 Click the row or column header for the destination data, go to the **Clipboard** section of the **Home** tab on the Ribbon, and click the **Paste** button. The contents of the original row or column are now pasted into the destination location.

Inserting Data

When you cut-and-paste data from the original row or column to the new location, all existing data in that new location is written over with the pasted data. This might not be what you want to do.

The alternative is to insert a new row or column to hold the data you've cut. When you use this approach you don't lose any data, nothing gets replaced, and all subsequent rows or columns are moved down or over to make way for the pasted data.

1 Click the row or column header for the row or column you want to move. Go to the **Clipboard** section of the **Home** tab on the Ribbon, and click the **Cut** button.

2 Click the row or column header for the destination location, go to the **Cells** section of the **Home** tab on the Ribbon, click the **Insert** button, and click **Insert Cut Cells**. This inserts a new row or column at the selected location and pastes the cut data into this location.

Hiding and Unhiding a Row or Column

Sometimes you put data into a spreadsheet that's necessary for calculations but not necessary to view. This happens a lot with larger spreadsheets, where not all the data present needs to be seen by all viewers.

When you want to unclutter a spreadsheet with nonessential information, you can take advantage of Excel's ability to hide selected rows and columns. When you want to see that data again, you simply unhide it.

Hiding a Row or Column

When you hide a row or column, you effectively resize it to a height or width of 0. The row or column—and all the data it contains—still exists and can still be referenced in formulas, but it's hidden from sight.

1. Click the row or column headers to select the row(s) or column(s) you want to hide.

2. Go to the **Cells** section of the **Home** tab on the Ribbon, click the **Format** button, select **Hide & Unhide**, and choose **Hide Columns** (or **Hide Rows**). The selected row or column is now hidden from view. If, for example, you hid column C, the column headers now read A, B, D, E—with column C hidden.

Unhiding a Row or Column

Anything you hide, you can unhide. When you need to reveal the contents of a hidden row or column, use Excel's unhide feature.

The primary challenge in unhiding a row or column is finding it—it's hidden, after all. The solution is to select the rows or columns surrounding the hidden one; the one you've hidden is in the middle.

1 Press and hold the **Shift** key, and click the row or column headers surrounding the row(s) or column(s) you want to unhide. For example, if you've hidden column C, press and hold **Shift** and select columns **B** and **D**. You'll select the hidden column C as well.

2 Go to the **Cells** section of the **Home** tab on the Ribbon, click the **Format** button, select **Hide & Unhide**, and choose **Unhide Columns** (or **Unhide Rows**). The hidden row or column is now expanded to full size and fully visible.

Freezing a Row or Column

Oftentimes, when you construct a spreadsheet, you place the data's column labels in row 1 of the sheet and the row labels in column A. This leaves the bulk of the spreadsheet available to hold your data.

If you have a lot of data in a lot of rows and columns, you might find yourself scrolling down the screen or to the right to view it all. The problem is, when you scroll down or over too far, you can no longer see your row and column labels—and you might forget what you're viewing or entering.

The solution is to freeze the rows and columns that hold your data labels. When you freeze a row or column, it's always visible on-screen, even if you scroll down or to the right a substantial distance.

Note you can freeze only rows at the top and columns on the left side of the spreadsheet. You can't freeze rows or columns in the middle of the workspace.

	A	B	
1	Region	Members	Dona
2	North	42	$ 50
3	South	32	$ 42
4	East	38	$ 45
5	West	41	$ 48
6			
7			
8			
9			
10			
11			
12			
13			

(Cell reference: A2)

1 To freeze one or more rows, select the row beneath those rows you want to freeze.

	A	B	
1	Region	Members	Dona
2	North	42	$ 50
3	South	32	$ 42
4	East	38	$ 45
5	West	41	$ 48
6			
7			
8			
9			
10			
11			
12			
13			

(Cell reference: B1)

To freeze one or more columns, select the column to the right of the columns you want to freeze.

	A	B	
1	Region	Members	Dona
2	North	42	$ 50
3	South	32	$ 42
4	East	38	$ 45
5	West	41	$ 48
6			
7			
8			
9			
10			
11			
12			
13			

(Cell reference: B2)

To freeze both rows and columns, select the single cell below and to the right of the rows and columns you want to freeze.

2 Click the **View** tab on the Ribbon, go to the **Window** section, and click the **Freeze Panes** button.

3 To freeze only the top row, click **Freeze Top Row**. To freeze only the first column, click **Freeze First Column**. To freeze more than one row or column, click **Freeze Panes**. A solid line appears beneath the frozen row(s) or to the right of the frozen column(s).

4 To unfreeze all frozen rows and columns, open the **View** tab, go to the **Window** section, click the **Freeze Panes** button, and click **Unfreeze Panes**.

> ✎ Note
>
> You can freeze just rows, just columns, or both rows and columns—as long as you do so at the same time. If you've already frozen row 1 and later want to freeze column A, row 1 will then be unfrozen. If you want to freeze both rows and columns, you need to do so in the same action.

Merging Two or More Cells

Not all cells in a spreadsheet have to adhere to the rigid grid of rows and columns. Excel enables you to merge several individual cells to create one large cell that spans multiple rows or columns (or both). This lets you create sophisticated visual grids for your data.

Merge & Center
Merge Across
Merge Cells
Unmerge Cells

! Caution

When you merge multiple cells into a single cell, only the data in the upper-left cell is retained. The data in all the other cells is lost.

 Select the cells you want to merge.

2 Go to the **Alignment** section of the **Home** tab, click the down-arrow next to the **Merge** button, and select **Merge & Center** (to center the text in the cell) or one of the other merge options listed.

Splitting a Merged Cell

You can separate, or split, any cells you've merged into a single cell. When you unmerge a cell, the data from the merged cell is placed in the upper-left resulting cell.

Note this only applies to cells you've already merged. You can't split an unmerged cell.

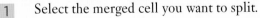

1 Select the merged cell you want to split.

2 Go to the **Alignment** section of the **Home** tab, click the down-arrow next to the **Merge** button, and select **Unmerge Cells**. The merged cell is split into individual cells to match the spreadsheet's natural grid.

Formatting Rows and Columns

Excel lets you apply similar formatting to all the cells within a given row or column. That way, you can format an entire row of labels or an entire column of subtotals. You can format an entire column of numbers with dollar signs and two decimal places or an entire row of numbers in bold red type. You even can format different types of data in different colors, by row or by column.

The key is to select the entire row or column and then apply the desired formatting. You can apply font formatting (font, font size, font color), cell formatting (color, border, and alignment), and number formatting to the selected rows and columns.

1 Click the row or column headers for the row(s) or column(s) you want to format. You can format multiple rows or columns at the same time.

Tip

To format more than one row or column, click the first row/column header, and hold down the **Ctrl** key while selecting subsequent rows/columns.

FILE	HOME	INSERT	PAGE LAYOUT	FORMULAS

A1   Region

	A	B	C	D	E	F
1	Region	Members	Donations	Pledged	Difference	
2	North	42	$ 500.00	$ 500.00	$ -	
3	South	32	$ 425.00	$ 400.00	$ (25.00)	
4	East	38	$ 450.00	$ 480.00	$ 30.00	
5	West	41	$ 480.00	$ 500.00	$ 20.00	
6						
7						

FILE	HOME	INSERT	PAGE LAYOUT	FORMULAS	DATA	REVIEW	VIEW

A1   Region

	A	B	C	D	E	F	G	H	I
1	Region	Members	Donations	Pledged	Difference				
2	North	42	$ 500.00	$ 500.00	$ -				
3	South	32	$ 425.00	$ 400.00	$ (25.00)				
4	East	38	$ 450.00	$ 480.00	$ 30.00				

2 Use the controls on the **Font**, **Alignment**, and **Number** sections of the **Home** tab to format the selected rows or columns.

Sorting Data

If you have a list of either text or numbers, you might want to reorder the list for a different purpose. Excel lets you sort your data by any column, either alphabetically or numerically, in either ascending or descending order. All you have to do is use Excel's Sort command.

Performing a Basic Sort

By default, Excel sorts based on the first column in the selected range. If you want to sort by a different column, or perform a more sophisticated multiple-column sort, you must use Excel's Custom Sort command.

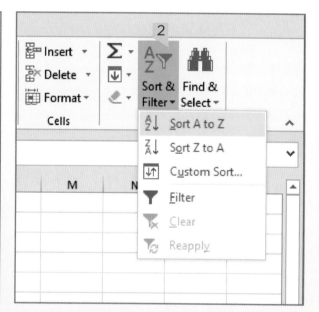

1 Select the range of cells you want to sort. If the data includes a row of column labels, include that row in your selection. Remember, Excel is going to sort on the data in the first column of the selected range.

2 Go to the **Editing** section of the **Home** tab and click the **Sort & Filter** button. To sort a column of numbers in standard order, select **Sort Smallest to Largest**. To sort a column of numbers in reverse order, select **Sort Largest to Smallest**. To sort a column of text in alphabetical order, select **Sort A to Z**. To sort a column of text in reverse alphabetical order, select **Sort Z to A**.

Creating a Custom Sort

Excel's basic Sort feature is nice, but what if you want to sort on the second or third column instead of the first one? What if you want to perform a multilevel sort, where you sort on one column first, then another column, and then maybe another?

When you want to perform more sophisticating sorting of your data, use Excel's Custom Sort feature. With Custom Sort, you can specify which columns you sort on—and even create fancy compound sorts on larger data sets.

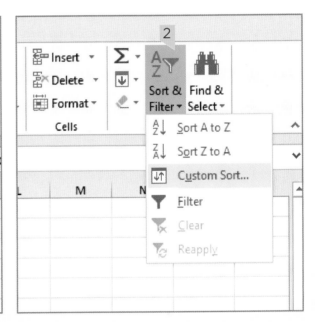

 Select the range of cells you want to sort. If the data includes a row of column labels, include that row in your selection.

2 Go to the **Editing** section of the **Home** tab, click the **Sort & Filter** button, and click **Custom Sort…**. This displays the Sort dialog box.

> **Tip**
>
> To undo a bad sort, press **Ctrl+Z** before attempting any other actions.

Creating a Custom Sort *(continued)*

3 If the selected range includes a row of column labels, check **My data has headers**. Excel then uses this header row to sort your data. If your data doesn't have a header row, it will use the standard column labels (A, B, C, etc.) to sort the data.

4 Pull down the **Column** list, and select on which column you want to base the sort.

Sort			? ✕
⁺ᴬ↓ **A**dd Level ✕ **D**elete Level ▣ **C**opy Level ▲ ▼ **O**ptions... ✔ My data has **h**eaders			
Column	Sort On	Order	
Sort by [Region ▼]	[Values ▼]	[A to Z ▼]	

OK   Cancel

5 Pull down the **Sort On** list, and select whether you want to sort on Values (the default), Cell Color, Font Color, or Cell Icon.

6 Pull down the **Order** list, and select how you want to sort. For numerical columns, you can sort from Smallest to Largest or from Largest to Smallest. For alphabetical columns, you can sort from A to Z or from Z to A. You can also choose a Custom List, which is useful if you're sorting by month or day of the week.

7 To sub-sort on additional columns, click the **Add Level** button to create a new "Then by" row in the dialog box.

8 Repeat steps 2 through 6 to tell Excel how to sort on this new column.

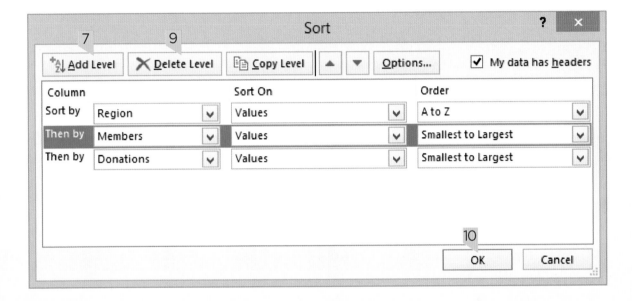

9 To delete a sorting column from this list, select that item in the dialog box and click the **Delete Level** button. To change the sorting order, select an item in the dialog box and click the up and down buttons to move it into a new position.

10 When you're done, click the **OK** button. Excel sorts your data in the order you specified.

Chapter 5

Working with Worksheets

An Excel workbook can contain multiple worksheets, each on its own tab. Each worksheet holds its own data and has its own unique look and feel. Excel can then reference other worksheets within any given worksheet in a workbook.

You can use multiple worksheets to contain different types of data required for a single project. For example, you could create a single workbook for a company budget but then create multiple worksheets with each department's individual budget.

Similarly, you can use multiple worksheets to contain similar data over time. You can use a single workbook to track your family budget and then assign individual worksheets for each year you're tracking. Just switch from one worksheet tab to another to view the yearly data.

In This Chapter

- Discovering how worksheets and workbooks work
- Configuring Excel's default number of worksheets
- Copying and moving worksheets
- Changing the name of a worksheet
- Changing the colors of worksheet tabs
- Deleting worksheets
- Grouping multiple worksheets in a workbook
- Viewing a worksheet in two panes
- Hiding worksheets in a workbook

Understanding Worksheets and Workbooks

It's time we got the nomenclature right. Many people refer to spreadsheets generically as "spreadsheets," but that's not a term Microsoft uses within Excel. In reality, a "spreadsheet" could refer to two different things.

A file you create in Excel is actually called a *workbook*. It's a "book" because it can contain multiple "chapters," or individual sheets within the main file. Each sheet, called a *worksheet*, is its own page of columns and rows. So what you've probably been calling a spreadsheet—and what we've called it, throughout the first part of this book—is more accurately called a worksheet.

Each workbook file can contain multiple worksheets, each on its own tab. By default, Excel labels the tabs Sheet1, Sheet2, Sheet3, and so forth, although you can rename any sheet you want. Click a tab to view that specific worksheet.

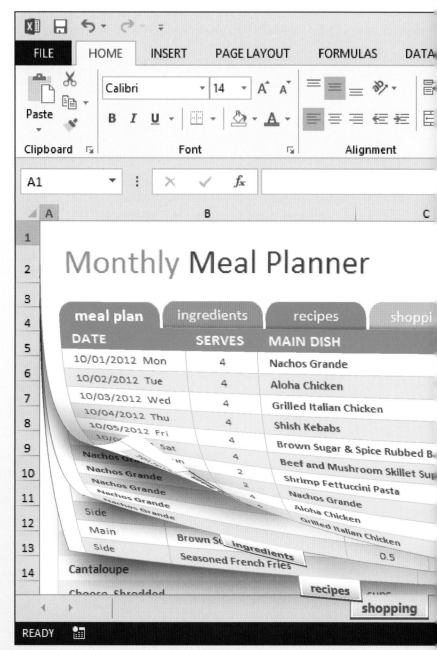

Why bother with multiple worksheets in a workbook? Multiple worksheets help you better organize your data. You can put different types of related data on different sheets but still keep them all organized in a single workbook.

For example, you might create a single workbook for all your business expenses but then put payroll, inventory, and other expenses on different worksheets within that workbook. You can then "roll up" your expenses on a final worksheet, referencing data stored on the other worksheets in the workbook.

Even better, Excel lets you format each worksheet differently, if you like. You might use different fonts or different colors on different sheets, depending on the type of data each contain. You even can change the order of the worksheet tabs in a workbook, group like sheets together for easier use, and hide those worksheets that contain background data you don't need to see for your daily work.

Navigating between worksheets in a workbook is a snap. All you have to do is click the tab at the bottom of the screen for the worksheet you want. And you can, at any time, add new worksheets to an existing workbook, or delete those worksheets you're no longer using.

Of course, you don't have to include multiple worksheets in a workbook. (Excel 2013 loads each workbook with just a single sheet, after all.) But if a given project requires varying but closely linked data—such as detailed company sales over multiple months or years—using multiple worksheets within a single workbook makes a lot of sense.

> **Note**
>
> If a worksheet is the tab or page of gridlines and a workbook is the file that contains multiple worksheets, just what is a "spreadsheet"? A spreadsheet is the type of program Excel is—that is, Excel is a spreadsheet program that creates workbook files filled with individual worksheets.

> **Note**
>
> By default, Excel 2013 workbooks are saved in the .xlxs file format. Prior to Excel 2007, the program saved files in the .xls format. Don't worry; Excel 2013 can open and edit files saved in the older file format. Excel 2013 can also read or import files in the .csv, .dbr, .dif, .ods, .prn, .slk, and .txt formats—although it can't save complete workbooks in most of these formats.

Creating a New Worksheet

When you create a new workbook, Excel includes a single worksheet in it by default. But you're not limited to that single worksheet. You can create as many more worksheets as you like. Each worksheet you create is contained on its own tab, and you can click a tab to view that worksheet.

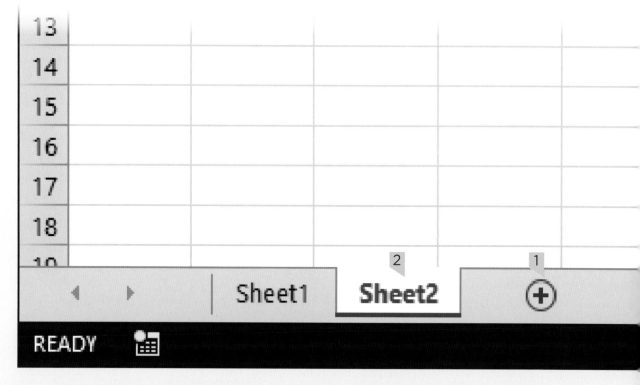

1. Move to the bottom-left side of the Excel window, and click the **+** button beside the right-most tab.

2. A new blank worksheet is added to your workbook on a new tab that appears to the right of the other worksheet tabs. The new tab is sequentially labeled Sheet*X*. If the last previous sheet was Sheet1, the new one is Sheet2. Click the new tab to view the worksheet.

Changing the Default Number of Worksheets

In Excel 2013, each new workbook contains a single worksheet, labeled Sheet1. If you'd prefer all your new workbooks contain more than one worksheet, you can change the default number of worksheets per workbook.

1   Select the **File** tab on the Ribbon, and click **Options** to display the Excel Options window.

2   Select the **General** tab on the left, and go to the **When creating new workbooks** section. Click the **Include this many sheets** control to select the number of default worksheets you prefer, and click the **OK** button.

> ✏ **Note**
>
> In previous versions of Excel, each workbook opened with three worksheets. The change to a single worksheet per workbook is new to Excel 2013.

Copying a Worksheet

Oftentimes, the best way to create a new worksheet is to make a copy of an existing one. That way, you use an existing sheet as a template for the new one, and you can replace the existing data in the copied sheet to get going.

When you copy a worksheet, the new worksheet has the same title as the original sheet plus a version number (in parentheses). So for example, if you copy a worksheet named Expenses, the new worksheet is named Expenses (2).

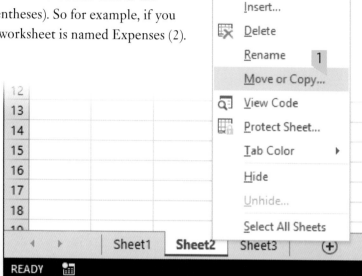

1 Right-click the tab for the worksheet you want to copy, and select **Move or Copy...**.

2 When the Move or Copy dialog box appears, check the **Create a copy** box. In the **Before sheet** list, select the sheet you want this sheet to appear before; if you want the copy to be at the end of your current worksheets, select (**move to end**). Click **OK**, and the new worksheet appears in the position you selected.

Moving a Worksheet

You can easily change the order of worksheets in your workbook by moving the tabs around at the bottom of the Excel window. This way, you can arrange your worksheets in the order that makes best sense for you.

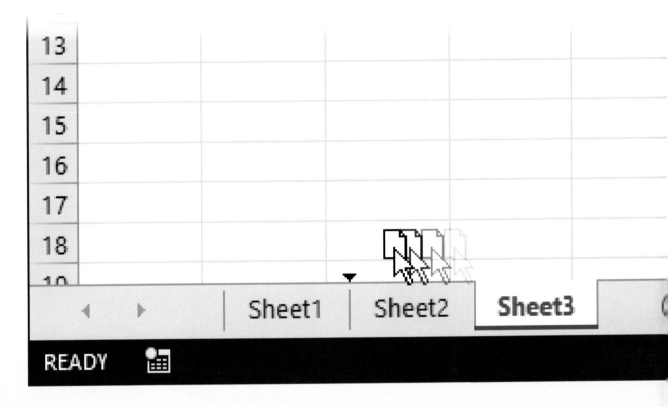

1 Click and hold the tab for the worksheet you want to move. The cursor changes to a small worksheet icon.

2 Drag the tab to the desired new position and release the mouse button.

Moving or Copying a Worksheet to a Different Workbook

Sometimes you have data in one workbook that might also be useful in another workbook. Excel lets you copy or move worksheets from one workbook to another easily. Copying the worksheet keeps a copy of the original in its original workbook; moving the worksheet removes it from the original workbook and pastes it into the other one.

To move or copy a worksheet to a different workbook, both workbooks need to be open on your computer. The resulting process is similar to copying a worksheet within a workbook.

1 In the original workbook, right-click the tab of the worksheet you want to copy, and select **Move or Copy...**.

2 When the Move or Copy dialog box appears, pull down the **To book** list and select the destination workbook. Select where you want the new worksheet placed in the **Before sheet** list. If you're copying the worksheet, check the **Create a copy** box; if you're moving the worksheet, leave the box unchecked. Click **OK** to complete the process.

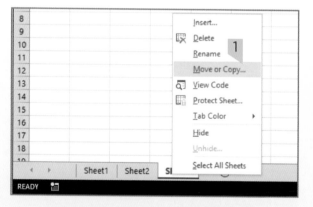

Renaming a Worksheet

Excel's default worksheet names are generic, which might prove less than totally useful. If you work with worksheets a lot, you'll want to rename the individual sheets to better reflect their unique content.

For example, if each worksheet in a workbook represents data from a different month, rename the sheets *January, February, March,* and so forth. If each sheet contains different types of household expense data, rename them *Groceries, Utilities, Automobile,* and the like.

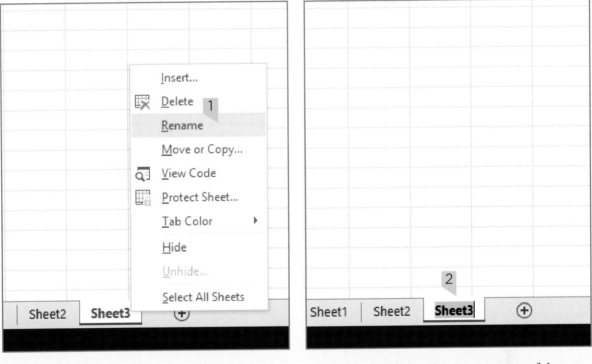

1. Right-click the tab of the worksheet you want to rename, and select **Rename**.

2. This highlights the current name of the sheet. Type a new name, which overwrites the former name, and press **Enter** when you're done.

Changing the Tab Color

When you want to better visually differentiate the different worksheets in a workbook, you can change the color of the tabs. Assigning different colors to different tabs not only looks more attractive but also helps you more easily find specific tabs.

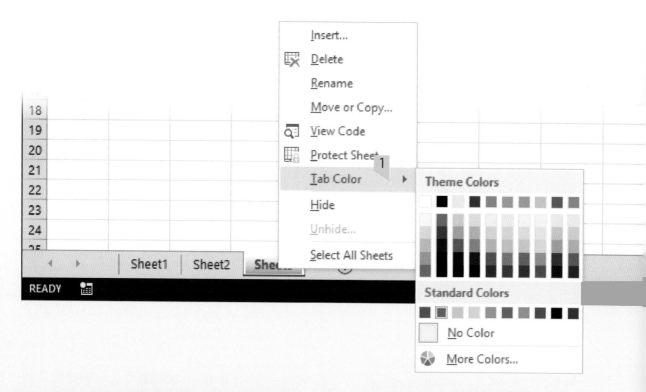

1. Right-click the tab you want to change, and select **Tab Color** to display the color palette.

2. Select a color from the Theme Colors or Standard Colors section, or click **More Colors...** to select a custom color from the Colors dialog box. Click **No Color** if you want to retain the standard coloring for the tab.

Deleting a Worksheet

If you find yourself with an empty or unused worksheet within a workbook, you can delete it. Know, however, that if you delete a worksheet that contains data, that data is deleted as well.

Insert...	
Delete	2
Rename	
Move or Copy...	
View Code	
Protect Sheet...	
Tab Color	▶
Hide	
Unhide...	
Select All Sheets	

Sheet1 Sheet2 **Sheet3** ⊕

READY

1 Right-click the tab for the worksheet you want to delete.

2 Click **Delete** from the menu of options.

> **! Caution**
>
> Deleting a worksheet deletes all the data contained in that worksheet. If cells in a deleted worksheet are referred to in formulas in other worksheets, those formulas will be affected.

Grouping Worksheets

3						
4						
5						
6						
7						
8						
9						
10						
11						
12						
13						
14						
15						
16						
17						
18						

◄ ► **Sheet1** Sheet2 **Sheet3** Sheet4 **Sheet5** Sheet6 ⊕

READY

In most instances, you work with a single worksheet at a time. However, for easier data entry, Excel lets you group multiple worksheets.

When you group worksheets, any changes you make to one worksheet are applied to all the worksheets in the group. For example, you might create a workbook for your company payroll, with different worksheets for each pay period. If you group the worksheets, you can add a new employee to one worksheet and have that employee automatically added to the others as well.

> **Note**
>
> Worksheet grouping applies only to the current Excel session. When you close Excel, any group you've created is lost. In addition, within your current session, if you select a worksheet that's not in the current group, all the previously grouped worksheets become ungrouped.

11					
12					
13					
14					
15					
16					
17					
18					

1 **2**

| ◄ ► | **Sheet1** | **Sheet2** | Sheet3 | **Sheet4** | **Sheet5** | Sheet6 | ⊕ | ⋮ |

READY

1 Click the tab for the first worksheet you want to include in the worksheet group.

2 Press and hold the **Ctrl** key, and click the tab for the next worksheet you want in the group. Keep the **Ctrl** key pressed as you continue to select additional sheets for the group.

3 Release the **Ctrl** key, and the worksheets are grouped together. Any changes you make to one sheet in the group are automatically applied to the other grouped worksheets.

4 To ungroup the worksheets, right-click any tab in the group and select **Ungroup Sheets**.

Insert...

Delete

Rename

Move or Copy...

View Code

Protect Sheet...

Tab Color ▶

Hide

Unhide...

4 Select All Sheets

Ungroup Sheets

13					
14					
15					
16					
17					
18					

| ◄ ► | **Sheet1** | **Sheet2** | Sheet3 | **Sheet4** | Sheet5 | Sheet6 | ⊕ | ⋮ |

READY

Splitting a Worksheet into Panes

What do you do when a worksheet contains so much data you can't view it in a single screen? As you scroll down or to the right, you lose sight of any data or labels in the top-most rows or left-most columns. The solution is to split the active worksheet window into multiple panes. Then you can scroll each pane separately, keeping visible the important parts at the top or left of the worksheet. Using panes enables you to more easily compare data located in different parts of the worksheet.

1 Select the cell whose top border marks where you want the horizontal division, and whose left border marks where you want the vertical division.

2 Select the **View** tab on the Ribbon, go to the **Window** section, and click the **Split** button.

> **Tip**
>
> Excel also lets you split the worksheet window into just two vertical or horizontal panes. To split into two vertical panes, click the cell in the first row of the column where you want the split, and click the **Split** button. To split the window into two horizontal panes, click the cell in the first column of the row where you want the split, and click the **Split** button.

Excel window screenshot showing the VIEW tab with the Split option enabled. The worksheet "Employee shift schedule1 - Excel" is split into panes showing a Shift Schedule.

The worksheet displays:

	A	B	C	D	E	F	J	K	L	M	N	O	P
1	Shift Schedule						For the Week of:		10/18/2017				
2							Department Name:						
3													
4	Monday	7:00 A.M.	8:00 A.M.	9:00 A.M.	10:00 A.M.		2:00 P.M.	3:00 P.M.	Sick?	TOTAL			
5	Kelly F	manager	manager	manager	manager		manager	manager		9			
6	Tom Y		cashier	cashier	cashier					4			
7	James S		front desk	front desk	front desk		front desk			7			
8	Jon M		front desk	front desk	front desk		front desk			7			
9	Sean P								Sick	0			
10	Teresa A						cashier	cashier		4			
36	Friday	7:00 AM	8:00 AM	9:00 AM	10:00 AM		2:00 PM	3:00 PM	Sick?	TOTAL			
37	Kelly F	manager	manager	manager	manager		manager	manager		9			
38	Tom Y		cashier	cashier	cashier					4			
39	James S		front desk	front desk	front desk		front desk			7			
40	Jon M		front desk	front desk	front desk		front desk			7			
41	Sean P								Sick	0			
42	Teresa A						cashier	cashier		4			
43													
44	Saturday	7:00 AM	8:00 AM	9:00 AM	10:00 AM		2:00 PM	3:00 PM	Sick?	TOTAL			

3 Excel now splits the worksheet window into four panes. Each pane contains its own vertical and horizontal scroll bars; use these scroll bars to navigate around that section of the worksheet. To resize a given pane, move your mouse over the appropriate dividing bar until the cursor changes shape, and click and drag the bar to a new position.

4 To remove all panes from the workspace window, just click the **Split** button on the **View** tab again.

Note

Excel synchronizes the vertical and horizontal scrolling of the split panes. The top vertical scrollbar scrolls both the top panes, and the bottom vertical scrollbar scrolls both the bottom panes. The left horizontal scrollbar scrolls both left panes, and the right horizontal scrollbar scrolls both right panes.

Hiding and Unhiding Worksheets

5					
6					
7					
8					
9					
10					
11					
12					
13					
14					
15					
16					
17					
18					

> **✎ Note**
>
> You can, if you like, hide the entire workbook in the Excel workspace. To do this, select the **View** tab on the Ribbon, and click **Hide** in the **Window** section. To unhide a hidden workbook, click the **Unhide** button.

Sheet1   Sheet2   **Sheet4**   Sheet5   ⊕

READY

At times, you might use a single worksheet within a given workbook to hold data you don't need to otherwise display. Maybe it's a kind of "scratchpad" tab, or just background data that's rolled up in more useful fashion to another worksheet in the workbook.

Because worksheets are designed to be flexible in meeting different users' needs, Excel lets you hide those worksheets you don't need or don't want to be visible. A hidden worksheet isn't deleted, it's just removed from sight. You can unhide it any time you need in the future. And you can still reference data in a hidden worksheet in other worksheets within the workbook. Just because it's not visible doesn't mean it's not usable.

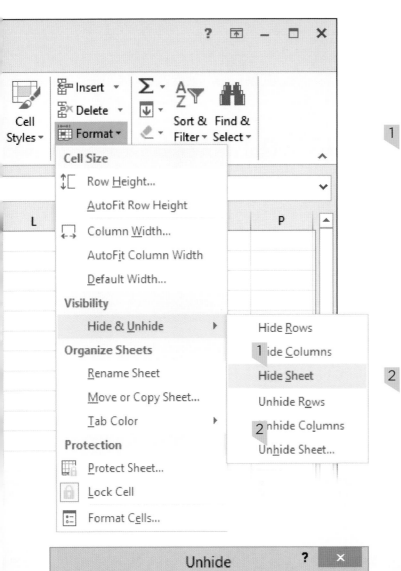

1　Click the worksheet you want to hide, go to the **Cells** section of the Home tab, and click the **Format** button. Select **Hide & Unhide**, and click **Hide Sheet**. The worksheet is no longer visible.

2　To unhide a previously hidden worksheet, go to the **Cells** section of the Home tab, and click the **Format** button. Select **Hide & Unhide**, and click **Unhide Sheet...** to display the Unhide dialog box.

3　Select the hidden sheet you want to display, and click the **OK** button.

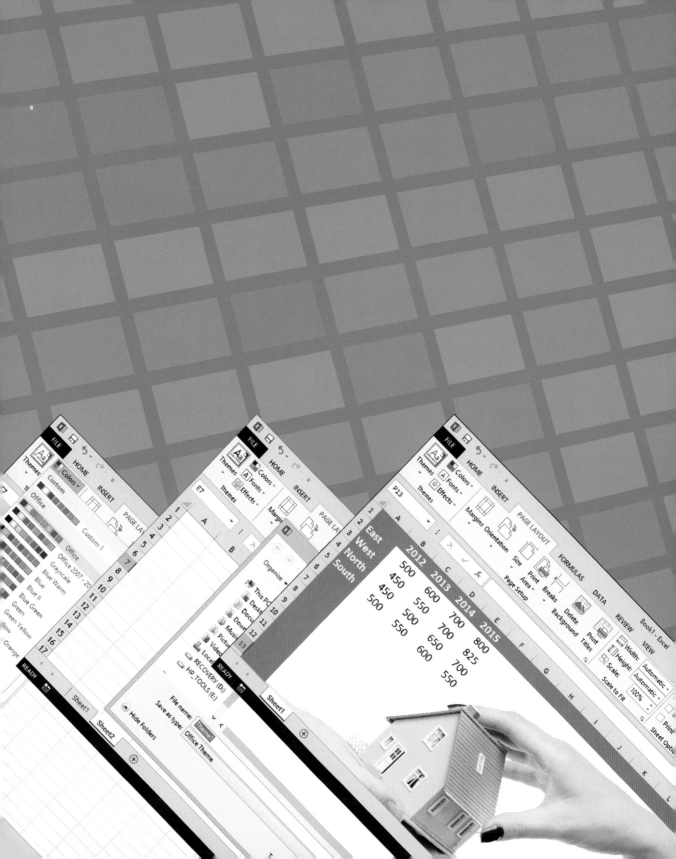

Chapter 6

Formatting Worksheets and Workbooks

As you've learned, Excel lets you format individual cells, rows, and columns to make specific data look visually unique within a worksheet. But what do you do if you want the worksheet itself—or all the worksheets in a workbook— to look different from Excel's default look and feel?

Excel makes it easy for you to format a worksheet or an entire workbook to look any way you want it to look. You can hide a worksheet's gridlines and row or column headings, add a background color or picture to a worksheet, or change the default font and colors for all the sheets in a workbook. You even can apply a workbook theme that uses a preset combination of fonts and colors. And let's not forget headers and footers, which can add useful information when printing.

Bottom line: you can make your worksheets look just about any way you like, which can spice things up a bit when you work in Excel.

In This Chapter

- Working with gridlines
- Showing or hiding row and column headings
- Formatting the background color of a worksheet
- Adding a background photo
- Copying formatting among worksheets
- Formatting the visual effects in a workbook
- Changing fonts and color schemes
- Applying a visual theme to a workbook

Changing Gridline Color

By default, Excel displays light gray gridlines in all worksheets. This gridline color is easy on the eyes and helps you focus on the data you enter. You can, however, change the color of the gridlines displayed on-screen for any individual worksheet or entire workbook.

1 Open the worksheet you want to format, select the **File** tab, and click **Options** to open the Excel Options dialog box.

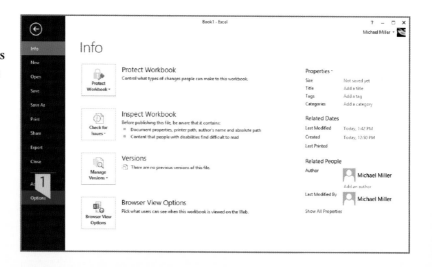

2 Select the **Advanced** tab on the left, and scroll to the **Display options for this worksheet** section. Pull down the list, and select the current worksheet, another worksheet in the workbook, or the workbook itself. Then click the **Gridline color** control, and choose a new gridline color. Click **OK** to see your changes.

Showing or Hiding Gridlines

Many users feel gridlines help them properly place data in cells. If you don't like to see all those fiddly vertical and horizontal lines on-screen, though, you can hide the gridlines for any individual worksheet in a workbook.

1. Open the worksheet you want to format, and select the **Page Layout** tab.

2. Go to the **Sheet Options** section, and uncheck the **View** box under **Gridlines**. (To redisplay gridlines, check the **View** box.)

> **Note**
>
> When you change the gridline color, or opt to show or hide gridlines, that only applies to what you see on-screen. Gridlines aren't shown when you print a worksheet, so however you format your gridlines doesn't affect the printed page.

Showing or Hiding Row and Column Headings

Just as you can hide gridlines in a worksheet, you also can hide a worksheet's row and column headings. Hiding these headings provides a much cleaner view of your work—even if it makes finding your way around a little more difficult.

1 Open the worksheet you want to format, and select the **Page Layout** tab.

2 Go to the **Sheet Options** section, and uncheck the **View** box under **Headings**. (To redisplay the headings, check the **View** box.)

> **Tip**
>
> By default, gridlines and row/column headers are not printed, so hiding the headers doesn't affect the printout. If you want to print gridlines or headers, you can. Go to the **Sheet Options** section of the **Page Layout** tab, and check the **Print** boxes for either **Gridlines** or **Headings**.

Formatting a Worksheet's Background Color

Black text on a plain white background is great for readability, but it can be a bit boring. If you'd prefer to see a different background color on-screen, you can change the fill color for all the cells in the current worksheet. And unlike gridlines, the background colors you choose *do* appear on printed worksheets.

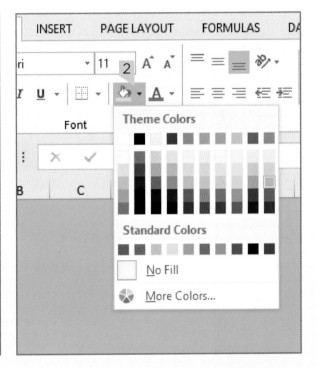

1. Open the worksheet you want to format, and click the **Select All** button at top-left corner of the worksheet, between the first row and column headings. This selects all the cells in the worksheet.

2. Go to the **Font** section of the **Home** tab, and click the down-arrow next to the **Fill Color** button. When the color chooser appears, select a background color. Something lighter is easier on the eyes when working with dark text.

Adding a Background Picture to a Worksheet

If you want your worksheets to look really special, you can place an image behind your spreadsheet data. A background picture works pretty much like the background images on your computer desktop; it doesn't affect your data at all, just puts the picture in the background while you work.

You can insert just about any image on a given worksheet. Excel lets you use images stored on your computer, on Facebook and Flickr, or elsewhere on the web (which you find using a Bing search). You even can use royalty-free clip art from the Office.com website.

Any background image you add to a worksheet only appears on-screen. Background images are not printed when you print a worksheet.

| P13 | ▾ | ⋮ | ✕ | ✓ | fx | |

	A	B	C	D	E	F	G	H	I	J
1		2012	2013	2014	2015					
2	East	500	600	700	800					
3	West	450	550	700	825					
4	North	450	500	650	700					
5	South	500	550	600	550					
6										
7										
8										
9										
10										
11										
12										

Formatting Worksheets and Workbooks

1 Open the worksheet you want to format, and select the **Page Layout** tab of the Ribbon.

2 Go to the **Page Setup** section, and click the **Background** button. This opens the Insert Pictures panel.

✎ Note

To remove an image from the worksheet background, go to the **Page Layout** tab and click the **Delete Background** button.

Insert Pictures

×

🖥 **From a file**
Browse files on your computer or local network

Browse ▸

🏢 **Office.com Clip Art**
Royalty-free photos and illustrations

Search Office.com

Ⓑ **Bing Image Search**
Search the web

Search Bing

•• **Flickr**
PhotopediaPhotos   Manage

See more ▸

Also insert from:

f

3 Select where the image you want resides: **From a file**, **Office.com Clip Art**, **Bing Image Search**, **Flickr**, **Facebook**, or **SkyDrive**. Search or browse for a specific image, select that image, and click the **Insert** button. The image is now downloaded and applied to the background of the current worksheet. If the image is smaller than the workbook area, it's repeated in a tile pattern across the screen or page.

Copying Formatting Between Worksheets

Once you have a worksheet formatted the way you like, you don't want to start over again when formatting other sheets in the same workbook. Fortunately, Excel enables you to copy formatting from one worksheet to another, which saves a lot of time and effort.

1 Open the worksheet that's formatted the way you like, and click the **Select All** button at the top-left corner of the worksheet, between the first row and column headings. Then click the **Format Painter** button in the **Clipboard** section of the Home tab.

2 Click the sheet tab to select the worksheet you want to copy the formatting to, and click the **Select All** button in the new worksheet. All the formatting from the first worksheet is now applied to the second one.

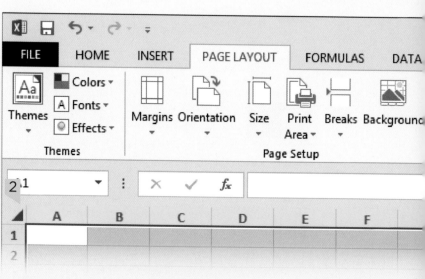

Applying Visual Effects to a Workbook

When you add graphics, shapes, or charts to a spreadsheet (which you learn how to do later), the objects you add can exhibit various visual effects. A shape or graphic can have a reflection, top or bottom shadow, glowing edges, glossy areas, or other effects. You apply these visual effects—or *theme effects* as Excel calls them—to lines, fills, and other components of selected objects like shapes, graphics, charts, and SmartArt. Some of these theme effects are subtle; others are less so.

Excel 2013 offers 15 different theme effects. These effects can be applied on a workbook-wide basis, as discussed here, or to each individual graphic you add, essentially overriding any previous formatting.

1   Select the **Page Layout** tab on the Ribbon, and click the **Effects** button to display a menu of options.

2   Select the visual effect you want to use in this workbook.

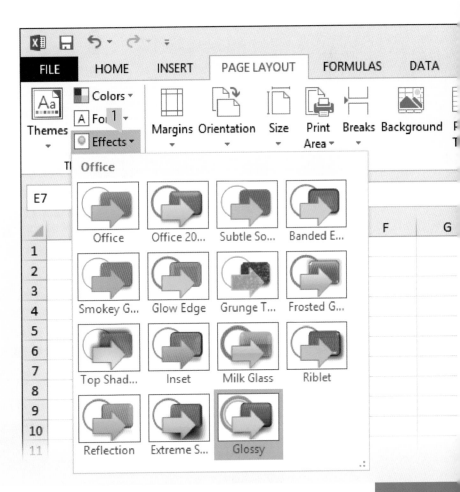

Changing Workbook Colors

When you want to change the color of text or cells in your spreadsheet, Excel offers a selection of theme colors you can choose from, along with Windows' standard system colors. These theme colors have been specifically designed to work well together in a spreadsheet and lend a coherent visual signature to your work.

An Excel color scheme consists of different colors for text, backgrounds, and accents. You can select from one of Excel's set color schemes or create your own custom combination of colors to use throughout the workbook.

1   Select the **Page Layout** tab on the Ribbon, and click the **Colors** button to display a menu of options.

2   Select the color scheme you want to use in the workbook

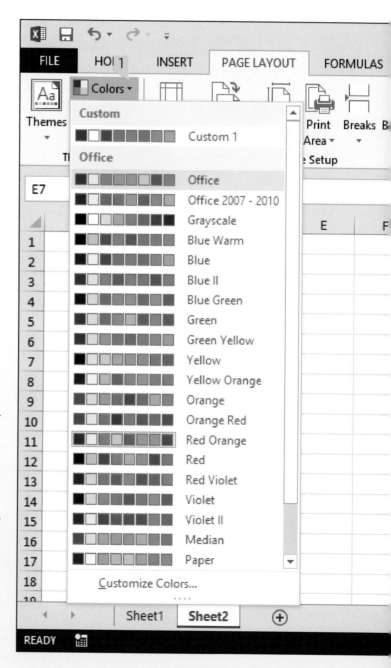

1. To create your own custom color scheme, click the **Colors** button on the **Page Layout** tab, and select **Customize Colors...**.

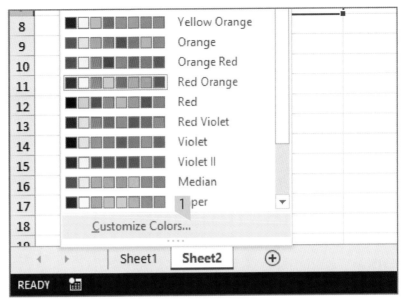

2. When the Create New Theme Colors dialog box appears, click each element in turn and select a color for that element.

3. After you have all your colors chosen, enter a name for your custom color scheme into the **Name** box to save it—and have it available on the Colors menu for other worksheets.

4. Click **Save** when you're done.

Setting Workbook Fonts

Every time you create a new workbook, Excel uses a default font for the data you enter—black 11-point Calibri. But what if you'd prefer something different, like 12-point Verdana or 8-point Times Roman, for example?

After you've created a new workbook or opened an existing workbook file, you can change the font used throughout all the worksheets in that workbook. So if you want your spreadsheet data displayed in Arial or Comic Sans, you can make it so. (Any formatting you do of individual cells is aside from the default font formatting.)

You even can change the default font used when you create new workbooks in the future. This won't affect existing workbooks, but will make all your new workbooks look exactly the way you want.

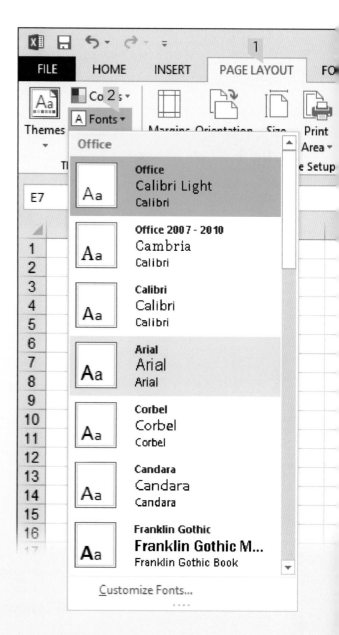

1   To change the fonts in the current workbook, start by selecting the **Page Layout** tab.

2   Go to the **Themes** section, and click the **Fonts** button to display the available font choices. Click a font to apply it to all the worksheets in this workbook. (This also changes the fonts used in the row and column headings.)

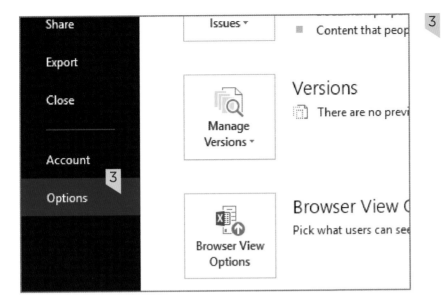

3 To change the default fonts for future workbooks, select the **File** tab and click **Options**.

4 When the Excel Options dialog box appears, select the **General** tab on the left and scroll to the **When creating new workbooks** section.

5 Pull down the **Use this as the default font** list, and select a new font. Then pull down the **Font size** list, and select a new font size. Click **OK** when you're done.

Applying a Workbook Theme

All the color, font, and visual effects you apply to a workbook can be combined into a unified workbook theme. When you apply a theme to a workbook, Excel applies all your preselected visual formatting to your workbook.

Excel 2013 comes with 29 built-in themes. You also can create your own custom themes.

1. Select the **Page Layout** tab on the Ribbon, and click the **Themes** button to display the available workbook themes.

2. Select the theme you want to apply to this workbook.

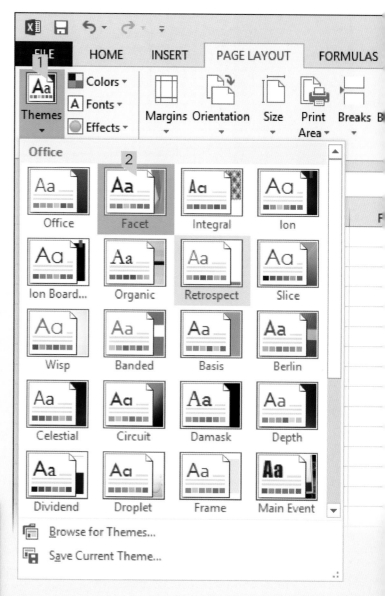

Note

You can apply an entire theme to all the worksheets in a workbook, or apply colors, fonts, and effects separately.

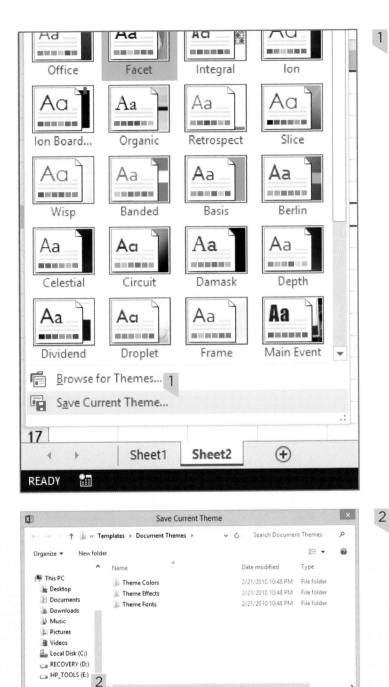

1 To create your own custom theme, start by applying an existing theme and then customizing the various font, color, and visual effect elements as you like. When the workbook looks like you want, open the **Page Layout** tab, click the **Themes** button, and select **Save Current Theme…**.

2 When the Save Current Theme dialog box appears, give the theme a name in the **File name** area, and click the **Save** button. Your new theme will now appear in the list of themes you see when you click the **Themes** button.

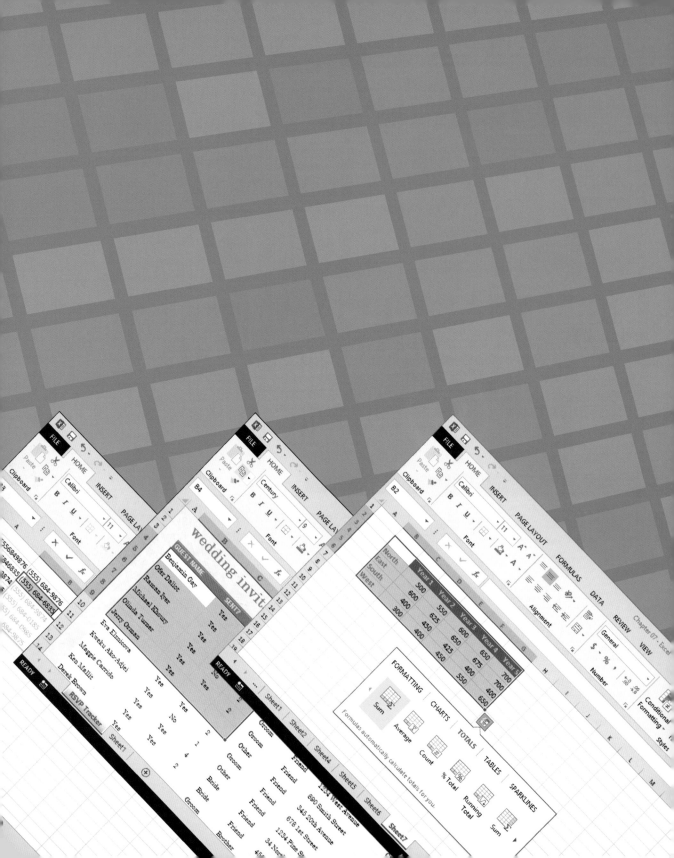

Working with Ranges

When working with a spreadsheet, it's often convenient to work with a group of cells as a single entity. When you group cells together in Excel, you create a range. You can name a range for easier navigation and for referencing in formulas. You also can copy, move, and delete an entire range in a single action.

Even better, you can easily format all the cells in a range at once and automatically fill a range of cells with similar or serial values. The key is treating a range as a single object, not a collection of individual cells. It really makes working with certain data sets much easier.

In This Chapter

- Selecting cells in a range
- Assigning a name to a range
- Using the Name Box to jump to a range
- Managing all the names in a worksheet
- Moving and copying ranges
- Deleting all the cells in a range
- Using AutoFill to automatically enter data
- Using Flash Fill to work with data
- Using Quick Analysis to format and analyze data in a range

Selecting a Range of Cells

A range is simply two or more contiguous cells in a spreadsheet. The range can consist of cells together in the same row, the same column, or some combination of adjacent rows and columns. Ranges are particularly useful when using formulas and functions, in that you can reference a single range by name as opposed to listing each of the cells individually. You can select the cells in a range with either your mouse or keyboard.

> **Tip**
>
> You can use a combination of mouse and keyboard to select a range as well. Use either your mouse or keyboard to select the first cell in the range, press and hold the **Shift** key, and click the mouse in the last cell in the range. All the cells between the two cells will automatically be selected in the range.

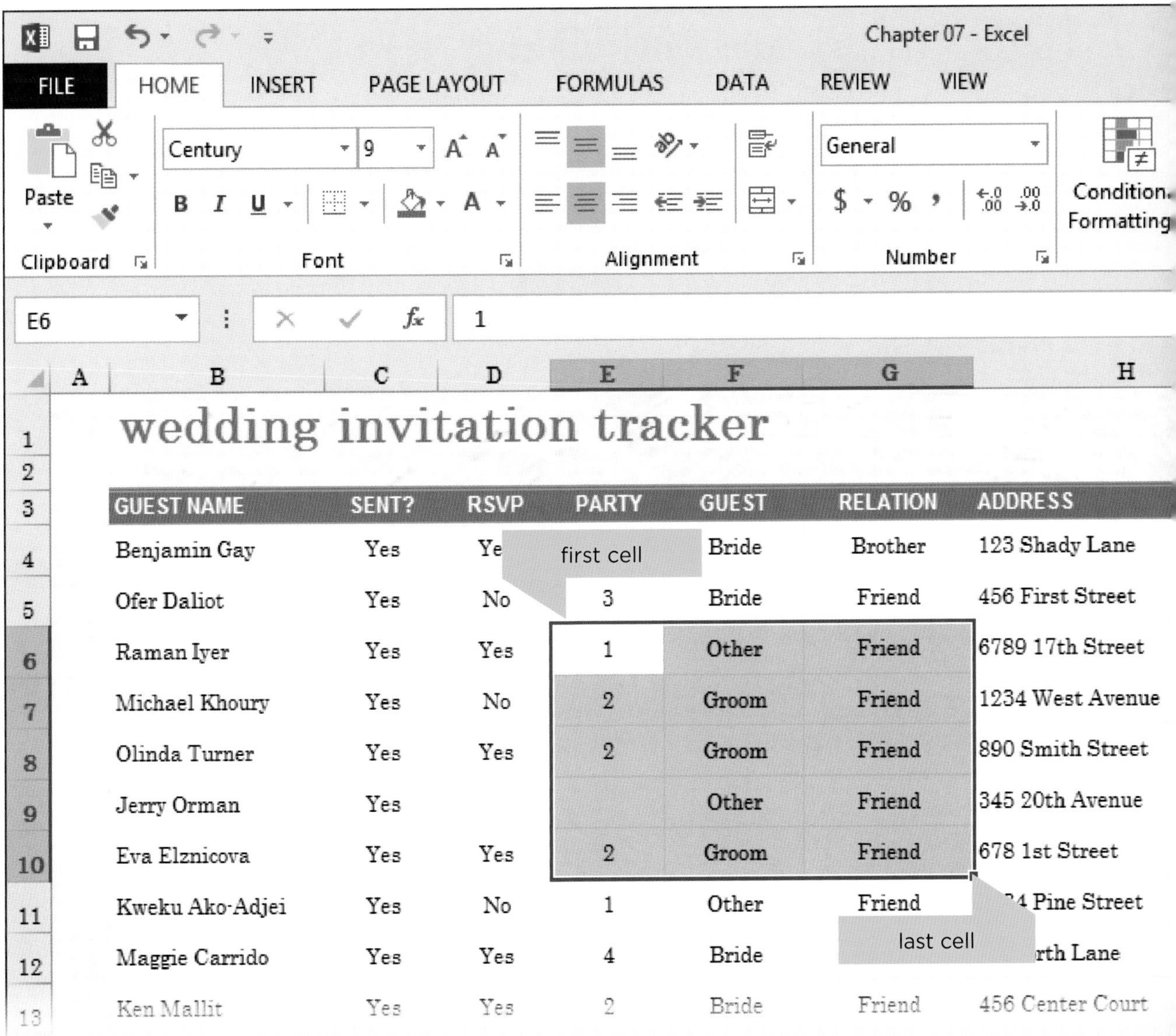

FILE　HOME　INSERT　PAGE LAYOUT　FORMULAS　DATA　REVIEW　VIEW

	Century	9	A A	≡ ≡ ≡ ≫	📄	General			
Paste	B I U		A	≡ ≡ ≡ �≡ ≡	📄	$ % ,	.0 .00	Condition. Formatting	

Clipboard　Font　Alignment　Number

E6　　fx　1

	A	B	C	D	E	F	G	H
1			wedding invitation tracker					
2								
3		GUEST NAME	SENT?	RSVP	PARTY	GUEST	RELATION	ADDRESS
4		Benjamin Gay	Yes	Ye	first cell	Bride	Brother	123 Shady Lane
5		Ofer Daliot	Yes	No	3	Bride	Friend	456 First Street
6		Raman Iyer	Yes	Yes	1	Other	Friend	6789 17th Street
7		Michael Khoury	Yes	No	2	Groom	Friend	1234 West Avenue
8		Olinda Turner	Yes	Yes	2	Groom	Friend	890 Smith Street
9		Jerry Orman	Yes			Other	Friend	345 20th Avenue
10		Eva Elznicova	Yes	Yes	2	Groom	Friend	678 1st Street
11		Kweku Ako-Adjei	Yes	No	1	Other	Friend	⁻4 Pine Street
12		Maggie Carrido	Yes	Yes	4	Bride	last cell	rth Lane
13		Ken Mallit	Yes	Yes	2	Bride	Friend	456 Center Court

1 To select a range of cells with your mouse, click the first cell of the range and hold down the mouse button. Drag the mouse down and/or to the right until all the desired cells are selected, and release the mouse button.

2 To select a range of cells with your keyboard, move to the first cell in the range, and press and hold the **Shift** key on your keyboard. Use the arrow keys to expand the range down and/or to the right. When you've selected the final cell in the range, release the Shift key.

Naming a Range

By default, Excel enables you to reference a range by its first and last cells, separated by a colon (:). For example, the range that starts with cell A1 and ends with cell B9 is written like this: **A1:B9**.

You also can assign your own custom names to a range, just as you can name individual cells in a spreadsheet. This makes it easier to reference cells in formulas, as well as navigate directly to a specific range of cells.

A range name must be a single word or phrase with no spaces. You can use letters, numbers, and selected special characters. You can use the underscore (_) to separate words without using spaces, like this: **first_range**. You can't use hyphens.

FILE | HOME | INSERT | PAGE LAYOUT | FORMULAS

Century | 9

B I U | A

Clipboard | Font | Alignme

Range1 | fx | Raman Iyer

range name

A | B | C | D | E

wedding invitation tra

range

GUEST NAME	SENT?	RSVP	PARTY
	Yes	Yes	1
Ofer Daliot	Yes	No	3
Raman Iyer	Yes	Yes	1
Michael Khoury	Yes	No	2
Olinda Turner	Yes	Yes	2
Jerry Orman	Yes		
Eva Elznicova	Yes	Yes	2
Kweku Ako-Adjei	Yes	No	1
Maggie Carrido	Yes	Yes	4
Ken Mallit	Yes	Yes	2

1 Select a range of cells.

GUEST NAME	SENT?	RSVP	PARTY	GUEST
Benjamin Gay	Yes	Yes	1	Bride
Ofer Daliot	Yes	No	3	Bride
Raman Iyer	Yes	Yes	1	
Michael Khoury	Yes	No	2	Groom
Olinda Turner	Yes	Yes	2	Groom
Jerry Orman	Yes			Other
Eva Elznicova	Yes	Yes	2	Groom

2 Select the **Formulas** tab on the Ribbon, go to the **Defined Names** section, and click the **Define Name** button.

Chapter 07 - Excel

ORMULAS   DATA   REVIEW

up & Reference ▾   ⊟ Define Name ▾   Trace Precede
& Trig ▾   𝑓x Use in Formula ▾   Trace Depend
Functions ▾   Name Manager   Create from Selection   Remove Arro

Defined Names

E   F   G   H

tracker

3 When the New Name dialog box appears, enter a name for this range in the **Name** box, and click **OK**.

New Name   ?   ✕

Name:

Scope: Workbook   ✓

Comment:

Refers to: ='RSVP Tracker'!$B$6:$G$8

OK   Cancel

Navigating with Range Names

Once you've named a range of cells, you can use that name to quickly go directly to the selected cells. It's a matter of using Excel's Name Box.

1. Enter the name of the range into the **Name Box** beneath the Ribbon.

2. Press **Enter** on your keyboard, and the named range of cells is now highlighted, with the first cell in the range selected.

	A	B	C	D	E	F
1		wedding invitation tracker				
2						
3		GUEST NAME	SENT?	RSVP	PARTY	GUEST
4		Benjamin Gay	Yes	Yes	1	Bride
5		Ofer Daliot	Yes	No	3	Bride
6		Raman Iyer	Yes	Yes	1	
7		Michael Khoury	Yes	No	2	Groom
8		Olinda Turner	Yes	Yes	2	Groom
9		Jerry Orman	Yes			Other
10		Eva Elznicova	Yes	Yes	2	Groom
11		Kweku Ako-Adjei	Yes	No	1	Other
12		Maggie Carrido	Yes	Yes	4	Bride

Note

You can enter either a range's custom name or cell reference in the Name Box for navigation. You also can enter the address of a single cell to navigate to that cell.

Managing Names in a Workbook

You use the Name Manager tool to manage all the names you've assigned to cells and ranges in a workbook. This tool enables you to edit, rename, and delete any names you've already assigned.

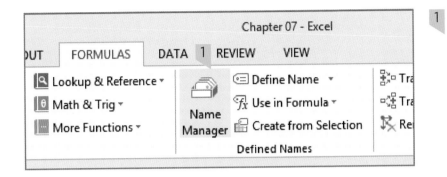

1. Select the **Formulas** tab on the Ribbon, go to the **Defined Names** section, and click the **Name Manager** button. This opens the Name Manager dialog box.

2. All the names you've defined in this workbook are listed in the Name Manager dialog box. To work with a name, select it.

3. To delete a name (but not the named cells or range), click the **Delete** button.

4. To edit cells included in a given name, click **Edit...** to display the Edit Name dialog box, and make the appropriate changes there.

Moving a Range of Cells

You can move a range of cells to another location in a worksheet, much the same way you move a single cell. When you move a range of cells, you move the cells themselves (they're cut and pasted) within the worksheet. No original data remains in the original location, as there is when you copy a range.

Replacing Cells

You can move cell ranges two different ways. The first approach replaces the destination location with the moved cells. Use this approach, and you overwrite all existing data, formulas, and formatting in the destination location.

1. Select the range of cells you want to move. Go to the **Clipboard** section of the Home tab, and click the **Cut** button.

2. Click the first (upper-left) cell where you want to move the range, go to the **Clipboard** section of the Home tab, and click the **Paste** button. (You don't have to select the entire destination range, just the first cell in the range.) The contents of the original cells are now pasted into the destination location.

> **⚠ Caution**
>
> Using this method to move a range of cells to another location completely deletes all the current contents of the destination cells, including all data, formulas, and formatting. If you want that data to remain, use the insert method instead.

Inserting Cells

The cut-and-paste method of moving ranges has one huge drawback—when you paste the cut data from the original range to the new location, all existing data in that new location is replaced with the pasted data. This might not be what you want to do.

The alternative is to *insert* a range of cells to hold the data you've cut. When you use this approach, you don't lose any data, nothing gets replaced, and all cells after this range are moved down or over to make room for the pasted data.

1   Select the range of cells you want to move. Go to the **Clipboard** section of the Home tab, and click the **Cut** button.

2   Click the first (upper-left) cell in the destination location, go to the **Cells** section of the Home tab, click the **Insert** button, and click **Insert Cut Cells**. This inserts a new range of cells into the selected location and pastes the cut data into this location.

Copying a Range of Cells

You can copy an entire range of cells to a new location within a worksheet. When you copy a range, the original cells remain in their original location as well as in their new location. This is different from moving a range, where the original cells no longer exist in the original location.

Deleting Data

There are two ways to copy a range of cells. The first approach pastes the copied data over any existing data, formulas, or formatting in the destination location.

1. Select the range of cells you want to copy, go to the **Clipboard** section of the Home tab, and click the **Copy** button.

2. Click the first (upper-left) cell in the destination location, go to the **Clipboard** section of the Home tab, and click the **Paste** button. (There is no need to select the entire destination range.) The contents of the original cells are now pasted into the destination location—and still remain in their original location as well.

original range

destination location

⚠ Caution

Using this approach to copy a range of cells to another location completely deletes all the current contents of the destination cells, including all data, formulas, and formatting. If you'd prefer to keep the data in the destination location, you'll need to use the copying method instead.

Inserting Cells

The copy-and-paste method of moving cells has the sometimes-unwanted side effect of overwriting all existing data in the destination range. That is, the cells you copy are pasted over existing cells, replacing whatever was there to begin with.

If there's no data in the destination range, this isn't a problem. If you want to keep the existing data in the destination location, on the other hand, you need to insert a new range of cells in which to paste the cells you've copied. This approach moves all other cells down or over to make room for the copied data.

1   Select the range of cells you want to copy, go to the **Clipboard** section of the Home tab, and click the **Copy** button.

2   Click the first (upper-left) cell in the destination location, go to the **Cells** section of the Home tab, click the **Insert** button, and click **Insert Copied Cells…**. This inserts new cells into the selected destination and pastes the copied data into this location.

Deleting a Range

When you need to delete several cells at once, the easiest way is to select all the cells and then delete the range in a single action. One action and all the cells are gone.

The problem you run into is that deleting a range of cells from the middle of a worksheet leaves a big hole that must be filled. So after you delete a range of cells, you must choose whether to shift cells beneath that range up or shift cells beside the range over to the left.

	A	B	C	D	E	F	G
1		wedding invitation tracker					
2							
3		GUEST NAME	SENT?	RSVP	PARTY	GUEST	RELATION	ADDRESS
4		Benjamin Gay	Yes	Yes	1	Bride	Brother	123 Shady
5		Ofer Daliot	Yes	No	3	Bride	Friend	456 First
6		Raman Ivan	Yes	Yes	1		Friend	6789 17th
7		Michael Khoury	Yes	No	2		Friend	1234 West
8		Olinda Turner	Yes	Yes	2	Bride	Friend	890 Smith
9		Jerry Orman	Yes				Friend	345 20th
10		Eva Elznicova	Yes	Yes	2	Bride	Friend	678 1st St
11		Kweku Ako-Adjei	Yes	No	1	Other	Friend	1234 Pine
12		Maggie Carrido	Yes	Yes	4	Bride	Friend	34 North
13			Yes	Yes	2	Bride	Friend	456 Cente
14		Derek Brown	Yes			Groom	Brother	2345 Hill

delete this range

shift these cells left

shift these cells up

> **⚠ Caution**
>
> Deleting a range of cells can wreak havoc on the formatting of a spreadsheet, as well as the construction of formulas that reference the deleted cells, so be careful when performing this action.

1 Use your mouse or keyboard arrow keys to select the range of cells you want to delete.

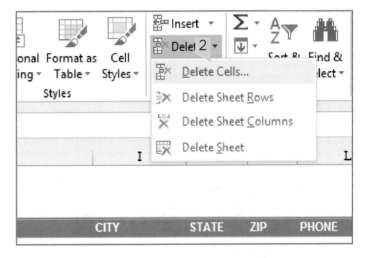

GUEST NAME		SENT?	RSVP	PARTY
Benjamin Gay	1	Yes	Yes	1
Ofer Daliot		Yes	No	3
Raman Iyer		Yes	Yes	1
Michael Khoury		Yes	No	2
Olinda Turner		Yes	Yes	2
Jerry Orman		Yes		
Eva Elznicova		Yes	Yes	2

2 Go to the **Cells** section of the Home tab, click the right-arrow next to the **Delete** button, and click **Delete Cells….**

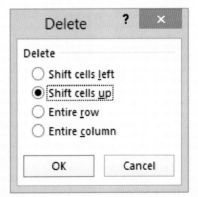

3 When the Delete dialog box appears, select which cells you want to move to fill in the space left by the deleted cells. You can choose to **Shift cells left** (from the right) or **Shift cells up** (from below). Click **OK** when you're done, and the designated cells move into place.

Filling a Range of Cells with AutoFill

Excel 2013 includes a feature called AutoFill, which lets you easily fill a range with data. You can duplicate a single value across selected cells, or let AutoFill automatically complete a series of values.

If the source cell contains a single number, AutoFill fills the selected cells with that number. For example, if the source cell contains the number **123**, all the auto-filled cells contain the number **123**.

If the source cell contains text, AutoFill fills the selected cells with the same text. But if the source cell contains text that Excel knows has meaning, it assumes that cell is the first in a series. For example, if the source cell contains the text **Jan**, the destination cells are filled with, in order, **Feb**, **Mar**, **Apr**, and so forth.

And if you select two more cells as the source, Excel determines if they represent a series and fills the destination cells with the next data in that series. For example, if you select two cells that contain the numbers **1** and **2**, the destination cells complete the series—**3**, **4**, **5**, and so forth.

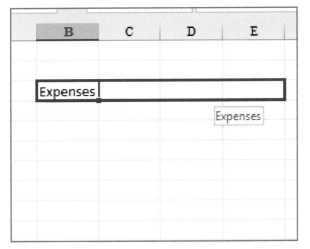

To automatically repeat data from a single cell, select that cell, and click and drag the fill handle (at the lower-right corner of the cell) down or over to select the destination cells. The data in the first cell is copied to the selected cells.

To automatically complete a series, select the two (or more) source cells at the beginning of the series. Click and drag the fill handle at the lower-right corner of the selected range down or over to select the destination cells. The series from the source cells continues in the selected cells.

After you've used AutoFill to complete the selected range, you can change what was copied into the filled cells. Click the **AutoFill Options** button at the lower-right corner of the destination range, and select from the following options: Copy Cells (repeats the data from the source cell or cells), Fill Series (completes the series started in the source cell or cells), Fill Formatting Only (copies only the formatting from the selected cells, not the data), or Fill Without Formatting (completes the series but retains the existing formatting for the destination cells). You also might have options for Flash Fill or other data-specific types of fills.

Flash Filling a Range

Excel 2013 includes a new feature not found in previous versions of the program called Flash Fill. Flash Fill analyzes data you've already entered and intelligently completes the balance of your data entry following the pattern of the existing data.

For example, let's say you've already entered a column of data containing both first and last names in each cell, but you'd also like to have first and last names separated into their own cells in separate columns. Excel doesn't let you split cells (you can only split previously merged cells), but you can use Flash Fill to do the work for you.

Just start a new column to the left of the current column, and enter the first name of the first person in the first row cell. Then start typing the first name of the second person in the second row cell, and Flash Fill shows a list of suggested names. Press **Enter** to accept the suggestion, and Excel fills the rest of the column with the first names of the people from the first column. Repeat this process in a third column to create separate cells for people's last names.

Similarly, you can use Flash Fill to combine columns. Using our same example, let's say you have two columns filled with names, one each for first and last names. Start a third column, and in the first row cell, enter the last name, add a comma, and enter the first name of the first person listed. Now enter the last name, a comma, and the first name of the second person into the second row cell, and accept Flash Fill's suggestion for the rest of the column.

Flash Fill works on more than names, of course. It kicks in whenever it recognizes a pattern in your data.

To reformat a column of data, create a new column to the right of the existing column. Enter data from the first column, first row cell into the new second column, first row cell, but formatted the way you want it. Now enter data from the first column, second row cell into the new second column, second row cell. Press **Enter** to accept Flash Fill's suggested fill of the second column.

A	B	C
5556849876	(555) 684-9876	
5556846835	(555) 684-6835	
5556849874	(555) 684-9874	
5556840185	(555) 684-0185	
5556840985	(555) 684-0985	
5556849875	(555) 684-9875	

To combine multiple columns of data into a single column, create a new column to the right of the existing columns. Enter the combined data from the first row of the original columns into the first row cell of the new column. Now enter the combined data from the second row of the original columns into the second row cell of the new column. Press **Enter** to accept Flash Fill's suggested fill of the new column.

A	B	C
FIRST	LAST	
Jonah	Jameson	Jameson, Jonah
Randolph	Scott	Scott, Randolph
Barry	Allen	Allen, Barry
Lew	Archer	Archer, Lew
Barney	Rubble	Rubble, Barney
Joyce	DeWitt	DeWitt, Joyce

To extract selected data from a selected column, create a new column to the right of the existing column. Enter the specific data you want from the first column, first row cell into the second column, first row cell. Now enter the same data from the first column, second row cell into the second column, second row cell. Press **Enter** to accept Flash Fill's suggested fill of the new column.

A	B	C
Address	State	
1234 First Ave, Burnsville, MN	MN	
9875 Goodlet, Indianapolis, IN	IN	
354 Grand Ave, Brooklyn, NY	NY	
1 Second St, Milwaukee, WI	WI	
34 Pacific, La Jolla, CA	CA	
685 Randolph, Portland, OR	OR	
54 N. Atlantic, Pittsburgh, PA	PA	
45 Main Street, Carmel, IN	IN	

Using Quick Analysis to Format or Analyze a Range

Quick Analysis is new to Excel 2013. This feature lets you apply conditional formatting to a range of cells. You can also use Quick Analysis to convert that range into a chart or table, calculate totals or averages for the data, and analyze the data via sparklines.

When you select a range of cells, a Quick Analysis icon appears at the lower-right corner of the selection. Click this icon, and Excel displays a gallery of available actions, depending on the type of data selected in the range.

2	Year 3	Year 4	Year 5
0	600	650	700
5	650	675	700
0	425	400	400
0	450	550	650

1 Select the range of cells you want to format or analyze.

2 Click the **Quick Analysis** icon at the lower-right corner of the selection to display the Quick Analysis gallery.

🕐 Tip

You can open the Quick Analysis tool from your keyboard by selecting a range of cells and then pressing **Ctrl+Q**.

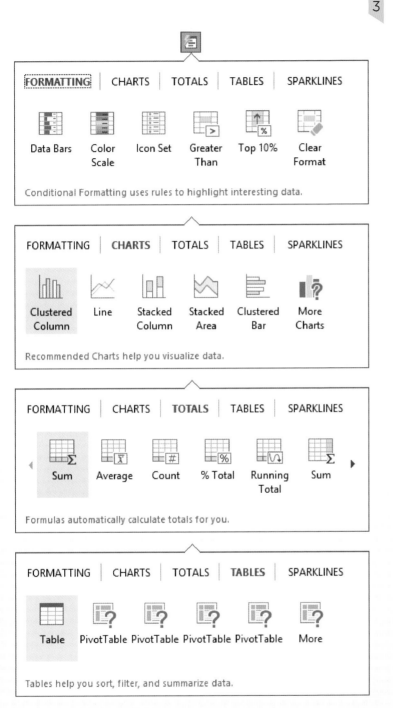

3 In the Quick Analysis gallery, you have a number of options:

- To apply conditional formatting to the selected range, select **Formatting** and make a selection. For example, you might want to add data bars or a color scale to visually differentiate levels of data.

- To create a chart from the data in the selected range, select **Charts** and select the type of chart you want.

- To calculate the data in the selected range, select **Totals** and select the type of calculation you want—Sum, Average, Count, % Total, Running Total, and the like.

- To create a table or Pivot-Table from the selected data, select **Tables** and make a selection. To analyze the data with sparklines, click **Sparklines** and select the type of sparkline you want to create. (More on tables, PivotTables, and Sparklines later.)

Chapter 8

Using Formulas and Functions

Once you've entered numerical data into a worksheet, you can build formulas that use the data you've entered to calculate values for specific cells. An Excel formula can use addition, subtraction, multiplication, division, and other operators, as well as references to other cells in the worksheet. For example, if you want to add the contents of cells A1, A2, and A3, you use the addition operator and references to the three cells, like this: **=A1+A2+A3**.

For more advanced calculations, Excel offers hundreds of built-in formulas called *functions* you can include in your formulas. Functions simplify the creation of complex formulas; all you have to do is insert the function instead of entering a series of complicated cell references and operations. For example, instead of adding cells A1 through A3 manually, you can use the SUM function to do the work for you, like this: **=SUM(A1:A3)**.

Formulas and functions, then, represent the real power of Excel. They're how you calculate and transform basic data.

In This Chapter

- Understanding how formulas work
- Entering and editing formulas
- Incorporating cell references in a formula
- Referencing ranges in a formula
- Pointing to other worksheets in a formula
- Using Excel's error-checking features
- Understanding how functions work
- Incorporating functions in a formula
- Working with the AutoSum, AVERAGE, and COUNT functions

How Formulas Work

Formulas enable you to perform calculations using the data entered into the cells of a worksheet. A formula can include the contents of specified cells, raw numbers, operators, and any of Excel's built-in functions. (More on functions later.)

The following table shows some typical Excel formulas you can use.

Typical Excel Formulas

In addition to these typical formulas available to you, you can construct your own. You use three elements to construct a formula in Excel:

- An equals sign (=), necessary at the start of each formula

- One or more cell references, or a specific number

- An operator to perform a specific action on the referenced cells or numbers

To create a formula, then, start with an equals sign and build from there.

You can use four types of operators when creating a formula in Excel—arithmetic, comparison, reference, and text.

Formula	Result
=5	5
=A1	The value of cell A1
=A1+A2	The value of cell A1 plus the value of cell A2
=A1-A2	The value of cell A1 minus the value of cell A2
=A1*3	The value of cell A1 multiplied by 3
=A1/3	The value of cell A1 divided by 3
=(A1+A2)/2	The value of cell A1 plus the value of cell A2, all divided by 2

Arithmetic Operators

Use the following arithmetic operators to calculate numerical results.

Operator	Description	Example
+	Addition	3+2
-	Subtraction	3-2
*	Multiplication	3*2
/	Division	3/2
%	Percent	30%
^	Exponentiation	3^2

Comparison Operators

You use comparison operators to compare two values. The result of such a comparison is either TRUE or FALSE.

Operator	Description	Example
=	Equal to	A1=B1
>	Greater than	A1>B1
<	Less than	A1<B1
>=	Greater than or equal to	A1>=B1
<=	Less than or equal to	A1<=B1
<>	Not equal to	A1<>B1

Reference Operators

You use reference operators to combine two or more cells into a range for use within the formula.

Operator	Description	Example
:	Range operator produces a single reference to all the cells between two cell references	(A1:B10)
,	Union operator combines multiple references into a single reference	(A1:A5,C2:C8)
(space)	Intersection operator creates a reference to cells common to two references	(A1:C10 B2:B5)

Text Operator

Excel offers a single text operator, the ampersand (&). Use the ampersand to connect or link two individual text values to create a single text value. For example, if you enter ="south"&"west" you get the result **southwest**.

Creating a Formula

Each formula you create is contained in an empty cell. The formula can reference cells adjacent to it or cells located anywhere in the worksheet.

Every formula starts with an equals sign (=), followed by the numbers or cell references you want to include in the calculation. Then you insert the desired operators between numbers or references, building the formula from left to right.

You can enter a formula directly into the selected cell, or type it into the Formula bar above the worksheet grid. When you're done entering the formula, the result of the formula is displayed in the cell. The formula itself is still displayed in the Formula bar.

formula in Formula bar

formula in cell

1 Move the cursor to the cell where you want to see the formula's results.

2 Enter an equals sign (=). This tells Excel you're entering a formula. Excel won't calculate formulas that don't start with an equals sign.

3 Type the rest of the formula into the cell. Remember to refer to specific cells by their location (A1, B2, etc.). Note that the formula is echoed in the Formula bar as you type.

4 When the formula is complete, press **Enter** or click the **Enter** checkmark next to the Formula bar to accept the formula (or press **Esc** to reject it). When you've accepted the formula, the results appear in the selected cell.

| FILE | HOME | INSERT | PAGE LAYOUT | FORMULAS |

Paste

Clipboard   Font   Alignment

SUM   × ✓ *fx*   =B3+B4+B5

	A	B	C	D	E	F
1						
2						
3		42				
4		63				
5		1 67				
6		=B3+B4+B5				
7						
8						
9						
10						
11						
12						
13						
14						
15						
16						

Editing a Formula

After you've entered a formula, you can edit it at any time. You can change, add, or delete cell references; change, remove, or add operators; and make the formula more or less complex, as necessary.

Excel lets you edit a formula within the cell itself or in the Formula bar above the worksheet grid. When you edit a formula, the referenced cells or ranges are highlighted in color in the worksheet.

formula in Formula bar

cells referenced in formula

	A	B		C	D	E
1						
2		Sales		Staff	Sales per Person	
3	North	$ 4,200		4	$ 1,050	
4	East	$ 6,750		6	$ 1,125	
5	South	$ 6,800		7	$ 971	
6	West	$ 4,620		5	$ 924	
7	TOTAL	$ 22,370		=C3+C4+C5+C6	$1,016.82	
8						
9						
10						
11						
12						
13						
14						
15						
16						

Formula bar: =C3+C4+C5+C6

1. Move the cursor to the cell that contains the formula you want to edit. The formula appears in the Formula bar.

2. To edit the formula within the cell, press **F2**. To edit the cell within the Formula bar, click anywhere within the Formula bar. The cells referenced in the formula are now highlighted in color within the worksheet.

3. Edit the contents of the formula as necessary. Remember to select entire cell references (A1, B2, etc.), not just a single letter or number.

4. Press **Enter** or click the **Enter** checkmark next to the Formula bar when you're done editing the formula.

Using Absolute Cell References in a Formula

| SUM | ▾ | ⋮ | ✕ | ✓ | *fx* | =$B$3-$B$4 |

	A	B	C	D	E	F	G	H	I
1									
2									
3		175							
4		124							
5									
6									
7				=$B$3-$B$4					
8									
9									
10									
11									

You can copy and move formulas from one cell to another within your spreadsheet using Excel's standard cut, copy, and paste commands. When you do so, however, the cells referenced within the formula shift along with the location of the formula. For example, if you have a formula in cell A3 that adds the contents of cells A1 and A2 (**=A1+A2**) and then copy that formula to cell B3, it no longer references cells A1 and A2. Instead, it now references cells B1 and B2 (**=B1+B2**). In this matter, cell references are *relative* to the location of the formula.

This might be exactly what you want to do—it's useful to copy an existing formula to perform that same calculation on a different range of cells, such as when you have similar columns of data you want totaled. In other instances, however, you want a copied or moved formula to continue to reference the original cells. In this instance, you need to use what Excel calls *absolute* cell references.

An absolute cell reference always refers to a specific cell location. The reference doesn't shift when a formula is copied; the reference is literally absolute. Absolute references are indicated by the use of the dollar sign ($) in front of the row or cell reference. You can create absolute references to columns, rows, or individual cells (combinations of columns and rows).

To create an absolute reference to a specific cell, enter a dollar sign before both the column and row reference. For example, to reference cell B3, enter **$B$3**.

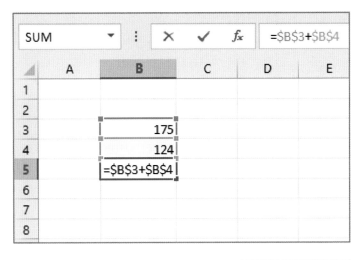

You can also create an absolute reference to any cell in a given column but keep a relative reference in regard to the row cells. You keep the column from changing if the formula is copied, even though the row references can change. To do this, enter a dollar sign only before the column reference, not the row reference, like this: **$B3**.

Likewise, you can create an absolute reference to any cell in a given row but keep a relative reference in regard to the column cells. You keep the row from changing if the formula is copied, even though the column references can change. To do this, enter a dollar sign only before the row reference, not the column reference, like this: **B$3**.

Using Ranges in a Formula

	A	B	C	D	E	F	G	H
	SUM	▾ ⋮ ✕ ✓ *fx*		=SUM(B3:B6)				
1								
2		Sales	Staff	Sales per Person				
3	North	$ 4,200	4	$ 1,050				
4	East	$ 6,750	6	$ 1,125				
5	South	$ 6,800	7	$ 971				
6	West	$ 4,620	5	$ 924				
7	TOTAL	=SUM(B3:B6)	22	$ 1,017				
8								
9								
10								

As you've learned, a range is a selection of adjacent cells in a worksheet. These cells may be in a single column, a single row, or a larger area consisting of cells in several columns and rows. A range reference is expressed by listing the first and last cells in the range, separated by a colon (:), like this: **A1:C4**. You can include ranges within your formulas. This enables a given operator or function to act upon all the cells within a range. When entered into a formula, the range reference looks like this: **=SUM(A1:A5)**. (This particular formula sums, or totals, the contents of cells A1 through A5.)

You also can use a named range or cell within a formula. After you've assigned a name to a given range of cells, simply enter that name into the formula in place of the traditional range reference. For example, if you assigned the name **WESTREGION** to cell B4, the formula **=B4*3** becomes the formula **=WESTREGION*3**.

Although this might seem like a lot of work, naming a cell or range creates an absolute reference to those cells. For example, if you'd referenced cell B4 but then sorted the cells within that range, the original formula would still refer to cell B4, even though the sort might have moved the cell contents to another location. By using a named cell or range, your formula always points to the same data, no matter where that data is in the worksheet.

When entering a formula, you can type in the range reference or select the range with your mouse or keyboard. To enter the range manually, enter the location of the first cell in the range, a colon (:), and the last cell in the range. For example, to reference the range starting with cell D3 and ending with cell D6, enter **D3:D6**. Excel highlights the range you've selected in the worksheet itself.

SUM	▾	⋮	✕	✓	*fx*	=AVERAGE(D3

◢	A	B	C	D	E
1					
2		Sales	Staff	Sales per Person	
3	North	$ 4,200	4	$ 1,050	
4	East	$ 6,750	6	$ 1,125	
5	South	$ 6,800	7	$ 971	
6	West	$ 4,620	5	$ 924	
7	TOTAL	$ 22,370	22	=AVERAGE(D	
8					
9					
10					

To select a range with your mouse, position the cursor within the formula where you want to insert the range. Use your mouse to move the cursor to the first cell in the range, press and hold the left mouse button, and move the cursor to the last cell in the range. This highlights all the cells in between. Release the mouse button when the entire range is selected, and the reference to that range is inserted into the formula.

D3	▾	⋮	✕	✓	*fx*	=AVERAGE(D3

◢	A	B	C	D	E
1					
2		Sales	Staff	Sales per Person	
3	North	$ 4,200	4	$ 1,050	
4	East	$ 6,750	6	$ 1,125	
5	South	$ 6,800	7	$ 971	
6	West	$ 4,620	5	$ 924	
7	TOTAL	$ 22,370	=AVERAGE(D3:D6)		
8					
9					
10					

> **⚠ Caution**
>
> If you enter a name in a formula and Excel displays the message **#NAME?** in the selected cell, you've either entered the name incorrectly or referenced a name that doesn't exist in your spreadsheet. Check what you typed, and reenter the name correctly.

Referencing Other Worksheets in a Formula

| | Clipboard | ☐ | | Font | | ☐ | | Alignment | ☐ | | Number | ☐ |

| SUM | ▼ | ⋮ | ✕ | ✓ | *fx* | ='Last Year'!D7 |

▲	A	B	C	D	E	F	G	H
1								
2		**Sales**	**Staff**	**Sales per Person**	**Prior Year**			
3	**North**	$ 4,200	4	$ 1,050	$ 900			
4	**East**	$ 6,750	6	$ 1,125	$ 1,133			
5	**South**	$ 6,800	7	$ 971	$ 1,042			
6	**West**	$ 4,620	5	$ 924	$ 1,125			
7	**TOTAL**	$ 22,370	22	$ 1,018	='Last Year'!D7|			
8								
9								

Here's something cool about Excel formulas—you're not limited to referencing cells in the current worksheet. You also can reference cells in other worksheets within the same workbook.

This opens some interesting possibilities. For example, you can put all your background data on one worksheet that you don't display publicly and then reference that data in calculations on a prettier, summary worksheet. Then you don't need to clutter your presentation worksheet with all those raw numbers.

The capability to reference data in other worksheets also helps you work with different iterations of selected data. Let's say you have a worksheet that contains 2012 sales data. You can then create a worksheet with 2013 sales data and reference the 2012 worksheet data as "prior year" numbers.

When you reference a cell in another worksheet, you precede the cell reference with the name of the worksheet and an exclamation point (!). For example, if you want to add cell D3 from a worksheet labeled June and cell C2 from a worksheet labeled July, the formula looks like this: **=June!D3+July!C2**.

> ✎ **Note**
>
> If the referenced worksheet name begins with a number or contains spaces, enclose the name in single quotes, like this: **'2012'!D2**.

1 You can insert references to other worksheets by hand by entering the name of the worksheet followed by an exclamation point, but it's easier to do so by pointing and clicking with your mouse. Begin by selecting the cell where you want the formula to appear, and enter = to begin the formula.

	A	B	C	D
1				
2		This Year Sales	Two-Year **1** Sales	Staff S
3	North	$ 4,200	=	4 $
4	East	$ 6,750		6 $
5	South	$ 6,800		7 $
6	West	$ 4,620		5 $
7	TOTAL	$ 22,370		22 $

◄ ► | **This Year** | Last Year | ⊕

2 Type the formula to the point you want to reference the cell in another worksheet. With your mouse, click the tab for the other worksheet, and click the cell you want to reference.

	A	B	C	D	E
1					
2		Sales	Staff	Sales per Person	
3	North	$ 3,600	4	$ 900	
4	East	$ 6,800	6	$ 1,133	
5	South	$ 6,250	6	$ 1,042	
6	West	$ 4,500	4	$ 1,125	
7	TOTAL	$ 21,150	20	$ 1,050	

◄ ► | **This Year** | Last Year | ⊕

3 The Formula bar displays the formula so far, including the reference to the other worksheet cell. Continue entering the formula and referencing other cells. (You have to click the tab for the original worksheet to reference other cells there.) Press **Enter** or click the **Enter** checkmark next to the Formula bar when you're done. Note that Excel automatically inserts worksheet references in front of all the cells referenced in the original worksheet.

⋮ ✕ ✓ *fx* ='Last Year'!B3+'This Year'!B3

B	C	D	E	F
This Year Sales	Two-Year Sales	Staff	Sales per Person	Prior Year
4,200	='Last Year'!B3	4 $	1,050	$ 900
6,750		6 $	1,125	$ 1,133
6,800		7 $	971	$ 1,042
4,620		5 $	924	$ 1,125
22,370		22 $	1,018	$ 1,050

Showing and Hiding Formulas

By default, Excel displays the results of a formula in the worksheet cell. To see the formula you've entered, select that cell. The formula is displayed in the Formula bar, and the result is shown in the cell.

You can opt to display formulas in cells instead. When you do this, the individual cells or ranges referenced in the currently selected formula are also highlighted in color.

	Trace Precedents	Show Formulas	
	Trace Dependents	Error Checking ▾	Watch Window
	Remove Arrows ▾	Evaluate Formula	

Formula Auditing

E	F

	=C3+C4+C5+C6	

B	C	D
This Year Sales	Staff	Sales
	4	=B3/C3
	6	=B4/C4
	7	=B5/C5
	5 2	=B6/C6
	=C3+C4+C5+C6	=B7/C7

1 Select the **Formula** tab on the Ribbon, and click the **Show Formulas** button.

2 All the formulas in the worksheet are now displayed within their cells. To hide formulas again (and display only the results of calculations), click the **Show Formulas** button again.

Checking for Errors in Formulas

If you've entered a formula incorrectly, you'll see a yellow warning diamond beside the formula when you select that cell; the cell itself displays **#REF!** or **#NAME!**. Fortunately, Excel offers an error-checking function that helps you troubleshoot any incorrect entries you've made and fix the broken formula.

1 Click the cell that contains an incorrect formula, select the **Formulas** tab on the Ribbon, and click the **Error Checking** button.

2 Excel displays the Error Checking dialog box. To work through the calculation step by step, click the **Show Calculation Steps…** button. To edit and correct the formula, click the **Edit in Formula Bar** button. To ignore the error and continue working, click the **Ignore Error** button. To move to the next cell that contains an error, click the **Next** button.

Understanding Functions

A function is kind of a mini-formula that simplifies the creation of more complex formulas. For example, although you could total multiple cells individually, by adding them together sequentially (=**A1+A2+A3+A4+A5**), Excel's SUM function gets the result more efficiently.

To use a function in a formula, you start with the standard equals sign (=), followed by the function, and then the function argument, in parentheses, which is typically a cell or range of cells. For example, to sum the range of numbers referenced earlier, you'd enter this formula with the SUM function: =**SUM(A1:A5)**. In essence, this function tells Excel to sum the range from cell A1 to cell A5. It's a lot easier than adding all five cells manually.

Excel offers hundreds of different functions, organized into 12 different categories, as described in the following table.

Excel Function Types

Type of Function	Description
Compatibility	Functions that have been replaced by new functions but are still available for compatibility with older versions of Excel
Cube	Functions for performing calculations and extracting data from a cube
Date and Time	Functions for returning or calculating date and time values
Engineering	Functions used in engineering scenarios, including for converting between measures
Financial	Functions for conducting financial calculations and analysis
Information	Functions that return information about the data in selected cells
Logical	Functions for Boolean operations (AND, OR, NOT), as well as conditional functions
Lookup and Reference	Functions that find or return references to cells and cell values
Math and Trig	Functions for performing mathematic, algebraic, and trigonometric calculations; for many users, these are the most-used functions
Statistical	Functions used in statistical analysis
Text	Functions for working with text strings (not numbers)
Web	Functions for converting data for use with and returning data from web services

Using Functions in Formulas

You can enter a function into a formula either by typing the name of the function or by pasting the function into the formula from those functions available in the Function Library section of the Formulas tab of the Ribbon. It's probably easier to enter simple or more-common functions manually, but use the Function Library to find and enter less-used functions.

1 To enter a function manually, go to the selected cell and enter **=** to begin a formula. Type the name of the function followed by an open (left) parenthesis, and enter the appropriate range or cell references.

2 Type a closed (right) parenthesis, and press **Enter** to complete the formula.

| FILE | HOME | INSERT | PAGE LAYOUT | FORMULAS |

fx Insert Function | Σ AutoSum ▾ | ? Logical ▾ | 🔍 Lookup & Refer◄
| ★ Recently Used ▾ | A Text ▾ | 6 Math & Trig ▾
| 🗏 Financial ▾ | 🕒 Date & Time ▾ | More Functions

Function Library

SUM ▾ ⋮ ✕ ✓ *fx* | =AVERAGE(D3:D6)

	A	B	C	D	
1					
2		**This Year Sales**	**Staff**	**Sales per Person**	
3	**North**	$ 4,200	4	$ 1,050	
4	**East**	$ 6,750	6	$ 1,125	
5	**South**	$ 6,800	7	$ 971	
6	**West**	$ 4,620	5	1 924	
7	**TOTAL**	$ 22,370		=AVERAGE(D3:D6)	
8					
9					
10					
11					
12					
13					
14					
15					
16					

1 To paste a function into a formula, go to the selected cell and enter = to begin a formula. Select the **Formulas** tab on the Ribbon, and go to the **Function Library** section. Click the button for the specific type of function, and select the function you want. (Your most-used functions are available in the **Recently Used** list.)

2 Excel now displays the Function Arguments dialog box. You can enter the referenced cell or range manually, or move back to the worksheet and use the mouse to select the cell or range. Click **OK** when you're done.

3 You also can browse or search for functions from the Insert Function dialog box. To display this dialog box, select the **Formulas** tab and click the **Insert Function** button.

Using the AutoSum Function

The SUM function is the most-used function in Excel. If you're like most Excel users, a good number of your formulas involve totaling rows or columns of numbers. Because this is such a common operation, Excel includes a one-button way to calculate simple totals, in the form of the AutoSum function.

When you click the AutoSum button on the Formulas tab, Excel inserts a formula (using the SUM function) in the cell at the end of a row or column of numbers. AutoSum attempts to determine which data is to be calculated, usually by selecting the contiguous range of numbers adjacent to the currently selected cell. If AutoSum selects an incorrect range of cells to total, you can still insert the correct range reference between the parentheses in the formula.

Caution

AutoSum merely suggests a range of cells to total. This range is not "official" until you accept the formula created. At any time before accepting the formula, you can manually select a different range of cells within the parentheses.

1 Select the cell to contain the calculation, preferably a cell at the end of a row or column of data.

	A	B		C	D	
1						
2		**This Year** **Sales**		**Staff**	**Sales per Person**	
3	**North**	$	4,200	4	$	1,050
4	**East**	$	6,750	6	$	1,125
5	**South**	$	6,800	7	$	971
6	**West**	$	4,620	5	$	924
7	**TOTAL**	$	22,370		$	4,070.43
8						
9						
10						

2 Go to the Editing section of the **Home** tab, and click the **AutoSum** button. You also can find an AutoSum button in the Function Library section of the Formulas tab, or press **Alt+=** on your keyboard to activate AutoSum.

AutoSum

Michael Miller

Insert ▾   Σ ▾   A▾Z
Delete ▾   ▾   Sort &   Find &
Format ▾   ▾   Filter ▾   Select ▾

nat as   Cell
ble ▾   Styles ▾

Cells   Editing

J   K   L   M   N

3 AutoSum now highlights a range of cells to be totaled. If this range is correct, press the **Enter** key or click the **Enter** checkmark next to the Formula bar to accept the formula and display the results of the calculation. If the range selected is not correct, use your mouse or cursor keys to highlight a different range, and accept the edited formula.

	A	B		C	D	
1						
2		**This Year** **Sales**		**Staff**	**Sales per Person**	
3	**North**	$	4,200	4	$	1,050
4	**East**	$	6,750	6	$	1,125
5	**South**	$	6,800	7	$	971
6	**West**	$	4,620	5	$	924
7	**TOTAL**			=SUM(C3:C6)	$	4,070.43
8						
9						
10						

Using the AVERAGE Function

If SUM is the most-used function in Excel, the AVERAGE function is a close number two. The AVERAGE function does just what the name implies—it averages the value in a selected range of cells.

For example, if you've entered the values **1**, **2**, and **3** into cells A1, A2, and A3, respectively and then enter the formula **=AVERAGE(A1:A3)**, the result of the calculation is **2**—the average of the values 1, 2, and 3.

1 Go to the cell where you want the result of the calculation to appear, and enter **=AVERAGE(**.

2 Enter the range of cells to be averaged. Alternatively, you can position the cursor and then use your mouse to select the cells. Type the closed (right) parenthesis, and press **Enter** to complete the calculation.

Using the COUNT Function

Excel's COUNT function is different from other functions in that it doesn't calculate values held in the referenced cells. Instead, it counts those cells within the referenced range that contain data. If a cell is empty, it isn't included in the count; only cells with data are counted.

For example, if you enter **=COUNT(A1:A3)** and only cell A1 contains data (that is, cells A2 and A3 are empty), the result of the function will be **1**.

	A	B	C	D	E	F	G	H	I	J
1										
2		This Year Sales	Staff	Sales per Person	Number Insured 2					
3	North	$ 4,200	4	$ 1,050	5					
4	East	$ 6,750	6	$ 1,125						
5	South	$ 6,800	7	$ 971	13					
6	West	$ 4,620	5	$ 924	1					
7	TOTAL				=COUNT(E3:E6)					
8										
9										
10										

Formula bar: **=COUNT(E3:E6)**

1 Go to the cell where you want the final count to appear, and enter **=COUNT(**.

2 Enter the range of cells to be counted. Alternatively, you can position the cursor and then use your mouse to select the cells. Type the closed (right) parenthesis, and press **Enter** to complete the calculation.

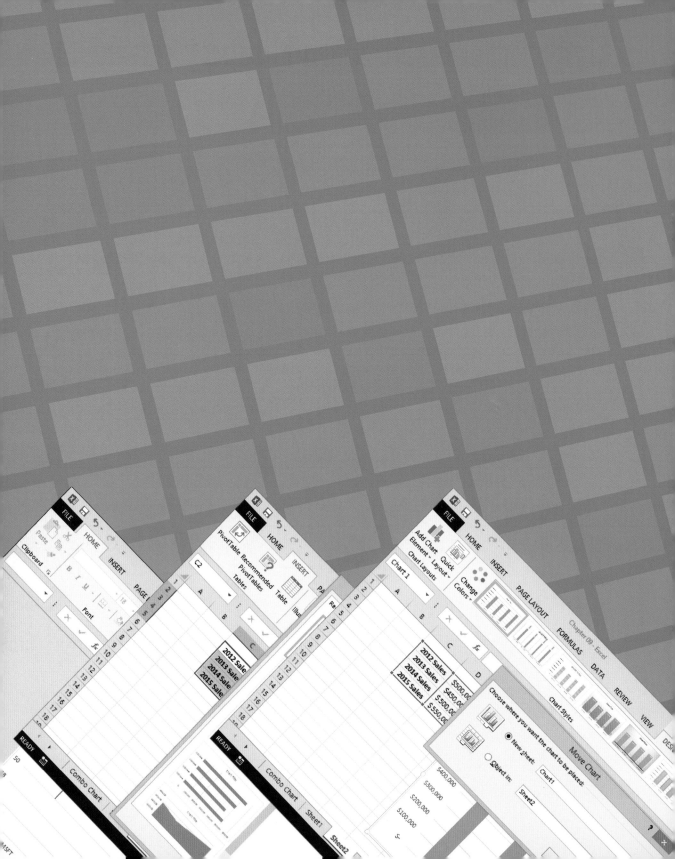

Chapter 9

Creating Charts

Numbers are great for presenting detailed information, but sometimes you just need to get the main point across—which for many people is better done visually. So when you want to show people what's important in your data, convert that data into a chart.

Simply put, a chart is a visual depiction of numeric data. Excel offers several different types of charts you can use to tell your story, including pie charts, area charts, line charts, bar charts, and scatter charts.

When you create a new chart in Excel, the chart can reside as a graphic on the current worksheet or on its own worksheet, called a chart sheet. Excel lets you create very sophisticated charts, but the basic process is actually quite simple—just highlight the range of cells to be charted and click the appropriate Insert Chart button on the Insert tab.

In This Chapter

- Understanding different types of charts
- Adding a chart to a worksheet
- Moving and editing your charts
- Showing and hiding chart elements
- Applying chart styles and colors
- Customizing a chart's axes
- Customizing tables
- Rotating 3-D charts
- Customizing the slices of a pie chart

Exploring Excel's Chart Types

What type of chart should you create? Excel provides tons of options, but certain types of charts are better at displaying certain types of data.

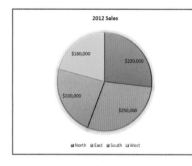

Pie Charts

A pie chart is best for showing the size of individual components proportional to the total. Each slice of the pie represents a given percentage of the whole. A pie chart can only express a single data series. (A doughnut chart is similar to a pie chart but can express more than one data series in multiple rings.)

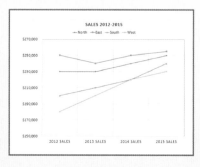

Bar Charts

A bar chart is best for comparing two or more individual items. Typically, the different categories or items you're comparing are on the vertical Y axis, with values along the horizontal X axis. Use a clustered bar chart to compare values across categories and a stacked bar chart to show the relationship of individual items to the whole.

Line Charts

A line chart is best for showing trends in data over time. Typically, time periods are displayed on the horizontal X axis, with values along the vertical Y axis. Use multiple lines to compare different items or categories.

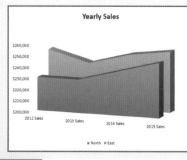

Area Charts

An area chart is best for expressing the magnitude of change over time. It's similar to a line chart but with the area beneath the line filled in. Typically, time periods are displayed on the horizontal X axis, with values along the vertical Y axis.

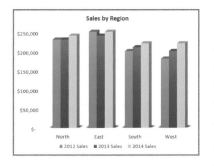

Column Charts

A column chart is best for showing how data changes over time, and for comparing two or more items. Typically, the different categories, items, or time periods you're comparing are on the horizontal X axis, with values along the vertical Y axis. Use a clustered column chart to compare values across categories and a stacked column chart to show the relationship of individual items to the whole. If you need to compare data points along two axes, use a 3-D column chart.

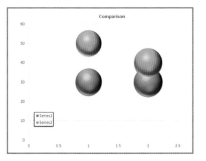

Scatter and Bubble Charts

A scatter chart (sometimes called an XY chart) plots one or more groups of data as a single set of XY coordinates and are typically used for scientific data. A bubble chart is a type of scatter chart that compares sets of three values along the XY axes, with the size of the bubble representing the third variable.

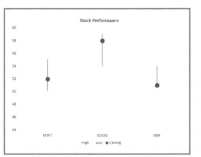

Stock, Surface, and Radar Charts

A stock chart is typically used to present high-low-close prices for stocks and other investments. A surface chart is like a topographic map, with different colors representing different ranges of values. A radar chart compares the aggregate values of a number of data series relative to a center point.

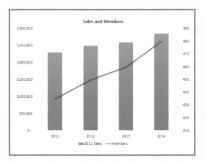

Combo Charts

A combo chart combines two or more chart types to best present disparate kinds of data and typically has two different Y axes, one on the left and one on the right, for the different types of data. For example, you can combine a column chart displaying one type of data over time with a line chart displaying a different type of data.

Creating a Chart

You create a chart from data you've already entered into a worksheet. By default, the chart is placed in its own graphic window on that worksheet, next to the selected data.

When you create a chart, Excel prompts you to select the type of chart you want. You can change the chart type, as well as format the chart to your liking, at any later time.

1 Use your keyboard or mouse to select the range of cells you want to use to create a chart. If the data includes row or column labels, include those cells in your selection.

2 Select the **Insert** tab of the Ribbon, go to the **Charts** section, and click the **Recommended Charts** button.

	A	B	C	D	E	F
1						
2			2012 Sales	$500,000		
3			2013 Sales	$450,000		
4			2014 Sales	$500,000		
5			2015 Sales	$550,000		
6						
7						
8						
9						
10						
11						
12						
13						
14						
15						

C2   2012 Sales

FILE   HOME   INSERT   PAGE LAYOUT   FORMULAS   DATA

PivotTable   Recommended PivotTables   Table   Illustrations   Apps for Office   Recommended Charts

Tables   Apps

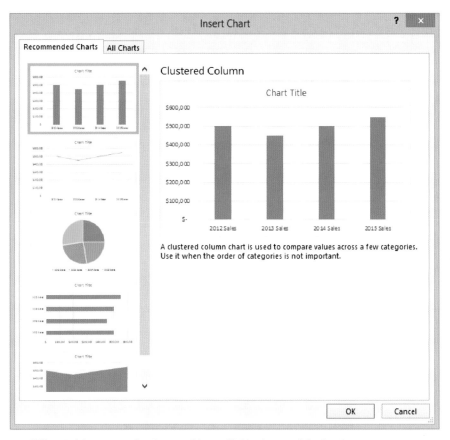

3   This opens the Insert Chart dialog box, with the **Recommended Charts** tab selected. Excel displays those charts that best fit the data you've selected. Click a chart to see it previewed (with your data) in the preview pane. Click **OK** to select and insert that type of chart in your worksheet.

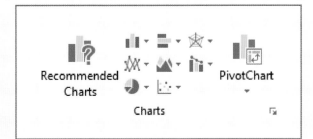

Alternatively, you can select a chart type directly from the **Charts** section of the **Insert** tab. Click the button for a given chart type to see all available subtypes, and click the chart you want. Excel creates the chart and inserts it in your worksheet.

Moving and Resizing a Chart

When Excel creates a chart, the chart is displayed in an image window on the original worksheet, next to the source data. You can keep the chart in this position or move the window elsewhere within the same worksheet. You also can make the chart bigger or smaller if you like.

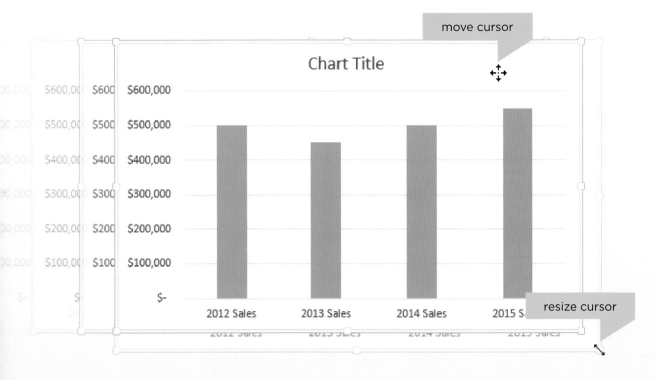

To move a chart window to a different location, mouse over the chart until the cursor changes to a four-arrow shape. Click and drag the chart to the new location, and release the mouse button.

To resize a chart, mouse over one of the four corners of the chart until the cursor changes to a two-arrow shape. Click and drag the corner of the chart window to make the window (and the chart) bigger or smaller, and release the mouse button. (To retain the original aspect ratio when resizing the chart window, press and hold the **Shift** key while dragging the corners of the chart.)

Moving a Chart to Its Own Chart Sheet

You can move the chart from its original worksheet to a completely different worksheet. A worksheet that exists solely to host a chart is called a *chart sheet*. You might want to use a chart sheet if you want to print your chart separate from its source data.

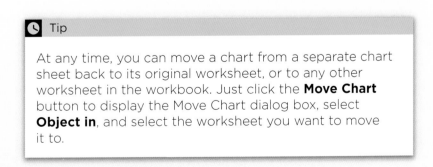

1 Select the chart to display a new **Design** tab on the Ribbon. Click the **Move Chart** button to display the Move Chart dialog box.

2 Check the **New sheet** option, and enter a name for the new sheet. (By default, Excel labels the sheet Chart1.) Click **OK**, and Excel creates a new sheet with the chart moved there.

> **Tip**
>
> At any time, you can move a chart from a separate chart sheet back to its original worksheet, or to any other worksheet in the workbook. Just click the **Move Chart** button to display the Move Chart dialog box, select **Object in**, and select the worksheet you want to move it to.

Changing the Chart Type

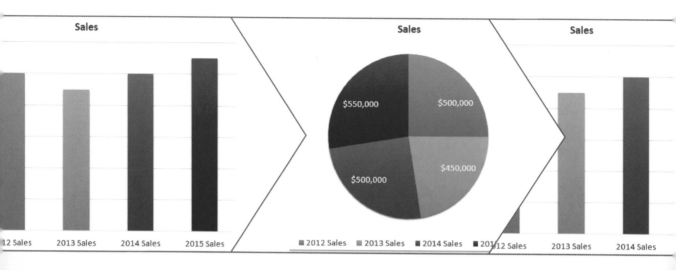

When you created a new chart, you also selected the type of chart to display. That type of chart might be fine, for now. But sometimes you start working with a chart and realize the data might be better presented using a different type of chart.

Fortunately, Excel lets you change the chart type at any time. So if you want to turn that line chart into an area chart, or that bar chart into a column chart, all it takes is a few clicks of the mouse.

1 Click to select the chart you want to change. This displays the Design and Format tabs on the Ribbon.

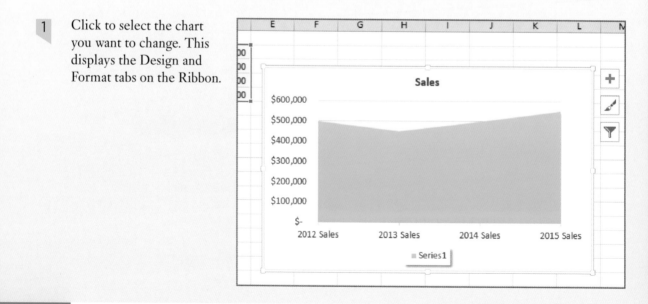

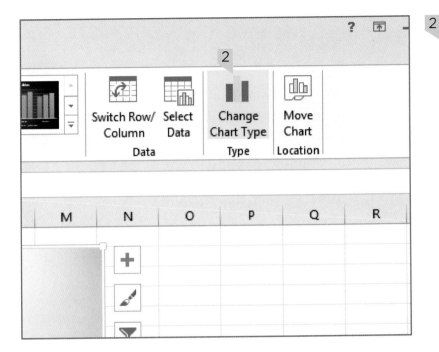

2 Click the **Design** tab, and click the **Change Chart Type** button to display the Change Chart Type dialog box.

3 Select the **All Charts** tab, and select the general chart type you want to use. Click the specific subtype you want, and click **OK**.

Changing a Chart's Source Data

Sometimes the data you use to create a chart changes. As you edit this source data in your worksheet, the chart based on that data automatically changes to reflect the new data.

However, you might decide the range of cells you selected to create the chart isn't quite right, and perhaps a slightly different range would create a better chart. (Or maybe you selected the wrong row or column to begin with.) To this end, Excel lets you change the source data selection—as well as swap rows and columns within the chart.

1 If your chart doesn't look quite right, it might be because the rows and columns of your source data are mapped to the wrong chart axes. To switch the row and column axes, click to select the chart, select the **Design** tab, go to the **Data** section, and click the **Switch Row/Column** button. The chart changes accordingly. (If you find this isn't what you wanted, click the **Switch Row/Column** button again to return to the original axes.)

2 To change the source data selected, click to select the chart, select the **Design** tab, go to the **Data** section, and click the **Select Data** button. This displays the Select Data Source dialog box.

3 To remove a row or column of data, uncheck that item in either the **Legend Entries (Series)** or **Horizontal (Category) Axis Labels** lists.

4 To add an additional row or column of data, click the **Add** button to display the Edit Series dialog box. To edit the source data range for either the vertical or horizontal axes, click the appropriate **Edit** button. This displays the Edit Series dialog box as well.

5 Within the Edit Series dialog box, enter (or use your mouse to select on the worksheet) the label cell for this range in the **Series name** box. Enter (or use your mouse to select on the worksheet) the data range into the **Series values** box. Click **OK** when you're done.

6 When you're returned to the Select Data Source dialog box, click **OK** to save your changes.

Adding and Removing Chart Elements

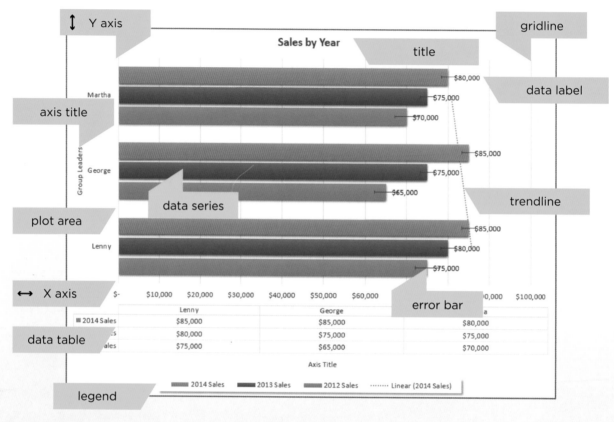

When you create a chart in Excel, it contains a few common elements by default. There are the data series, presented as bars, columns, lines, or whatnot. There are the X and Y axes (for most charts), which contain text describing the values presented. Most charts feature horizontal gridlines to help viewers better see data values. And of course, you have the plot area (the background behind the chart data) and the chart area (the entire chart window).

Excel offers several other elements you can add to a chart. You can opt to display axis titles, data labels, a data table underneath the chart, a legend for the various data series, and trendlines and error bars for further data analysis.

You also can opt not to display several of the included elements. The only elements you can't display are the data series themselves along with the plot and chart areas.

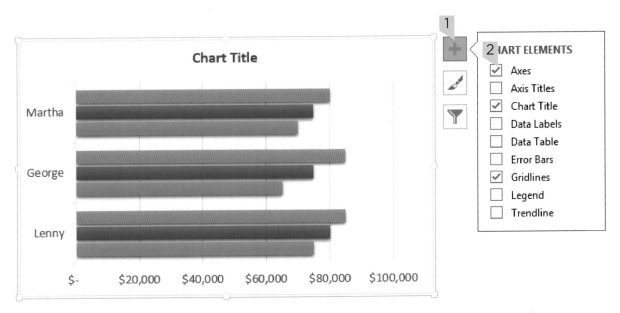

1 In Excel 2013, the easiest way to determine which chart elements to display is to select the chart and then click the **Chart Elements** (+) button to the right side of the chart.

2 This displays the Chart Elements panel. Check those items you want to display, and uncheck those you don't want to see in your chart. As you check and uncheck items, your selections change the appearance of the chart. Hide the Chart Elements panel by clicking the **Chart Elements** button again.

> **Tip**
>
> In general, charts that are visually simpler are easier to comprehend. It's tempting to add data labels, data tables, legends, and the like, but they tend to clutter the presentation and draw the eye away from the important data. So if you include data labels (to display discrete data values), you don't need to duplicate that information in a data table—or vice versa. Keep it simple to better get your point across.

Changing Chart Style and Color

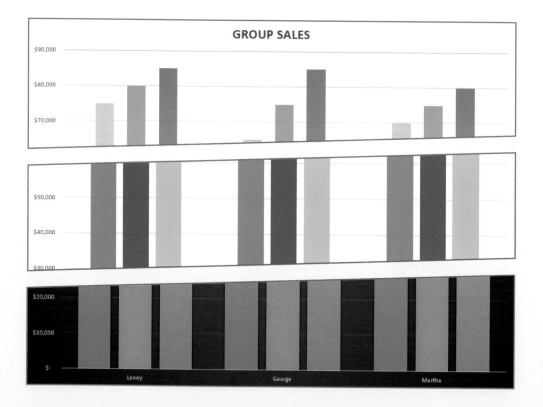

The chart Excel automatically creates from your data is very much a plain-vanilla chart. Not surprisingly, Excel lets you customize the way your chart looks, in a number of different ways. The easiest way to change a chart's appearance is to select from Excel's built-in styles and color schemes. A style describes the total visual appearance of the chart, including the use of background color, fonts for text elements, and the like. A color scheme determines which complementary colors are used for the bars, columns, and lines of the chart.

You can change chart style and color in two ways. You can use the Chart Styles button and corresponding panel that appears on the right side of the selected chart, or you can use the similar controls that appear in the Chart Styles section of the Design tab on the Ribbon.

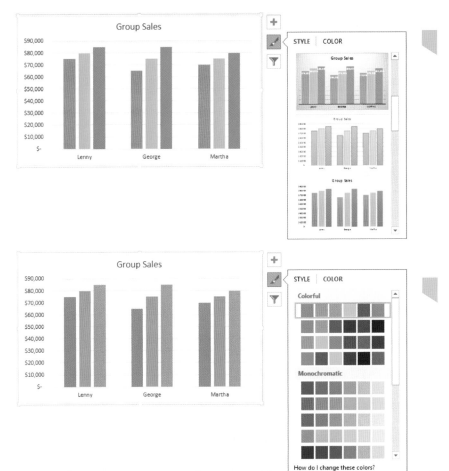

To change the chart style, select the chart, and click the **Chart Styles** button that appears to the right of the chart. When the options pane appears, select the **Style** tab to view all available styles. Click the style you want to apply.

To change the color scheme, click the **Chart Styles** button to display the options pane, and select the **Colors** tab to view all available color schemes. Click the color scheme you want to apply.

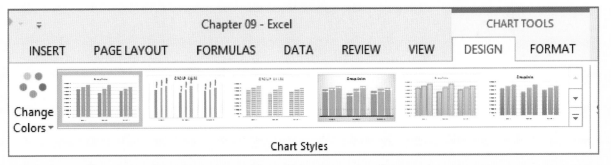

You can also change styles and colors from the Design tab on the Ribbon. Click to select the chart, and the Design tab displays. Select the **Design** tab, and go to the **Chart Styles** section. Click to select one of the available chart styles, or click the **Change Colors** button to select a different color scheme.

Formatting Chart Elements

The quickest and easiest way to format a chart is to use Excel's built-in styles and color schemes, but you can perform even more customization if you want. In fact, you can format just about any part of the chart you want, from the largest object to the shortest line.

Each element in your chart has its own distinct formatting options. Depending on the element, you may be able to change fill color, border type and color, visual effects, even the width and depth of the bars and columns in a chart.

Despite the different options, the way you format chart elements is the same no matter which element you're formatting. It's a matter of selecting the element and displaying that specific Format pane. All the available formatting options are available there.

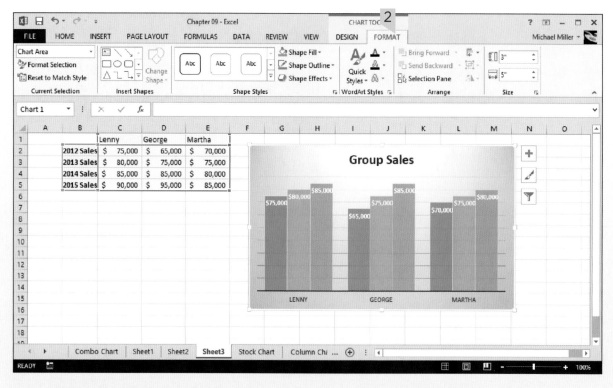

1 Click to select the chart you want to format. This displays the Design and Format tabs on the Ribbon.

2 Select the **Format** tab.

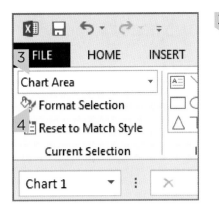

3 Go to the **Current Selection** section, pull down the list of elements, and select the element you want to format. Alternatively, you can double-click that element within the chart itself.

4 Click the **Format Selection** button in the Current Selection section of the Format ribbon.

5

Format Chart Area

CHART OPTIONS ▾ | TEXT OPTIONS

▷ **FILL**

▲ **BORDER**

○ No line
○ Solid line
○ Gradient line
● Automatic

Color
Transparency |——— 0%
Width 0.75 pt
Compound type

Group Sales

$85,000
$75,000
$65,000
$70,000 $75,000 $80,000

GEORGE   MARTHA

5 This displays a Format panel beside the chart in your worksheet. All the formatting options for that element are listed here, so you can configure the formatting as you want. Click the **X** to close the Format panel.

Formatting the Chart Area

You can format any individual element in a given chart. Let's start by formatting the chart area itself—essentially, everything inside the chart window. You can change the fill color of the area, apply various visual effects, even change the color of all text used in your chart.

To format the chart area, select **Chart Area** as the current selection on the Format tab, and click the **Format Selection** button to display the Format Chart Area panel.

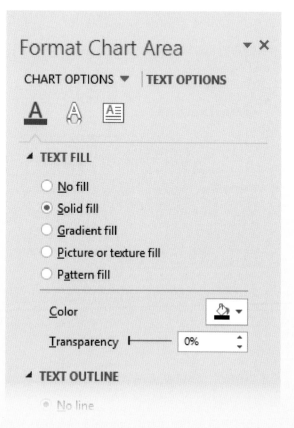

To format nontext elements in the chart window, select the **Chart Options** tab. From here, click one of the three icons to configure **Fill & Line**, **Effects**, or **Size & Properties** options, respectively. For each selected item, scroll down to see all available formatting options. Click an option to see it applied to your chart.

To format all the text in the chart window, select the **Text Options** tab. From here, click one of the three icons to configure **Text Fill & Outline**, **Text Effects**, or **Textbox** options, respectively. For each selected item, scroll down to see all available formatting options. Click an option to apply it to all the text in your chart.

Formatting the Plot Area

The plot area is that part of the chart window behind the data series—essentially, the background of the chart. (But not the background of the entire chart window.) You can format the fill color, border type and color, and special effects applied to the plot area.

To format the plot area, select **Plot Area** as the current selection on the Format tab, and click the **Format Selection** button to display the Format Plot Area panel.

To format the background color and borders of the plot area, click the **Fill & Line** icon. From here you can select different types of fills and fill colors, as well as different border styles and colors.

To apply various visual effects, click the **Effects** icon. From here you can configure shadow, glow, and soft edge effects. In 3-D charts, you can also configure 3-D format and rotation.

Formatting Axes

For most chart types (pie charts being a notable exception), Excel displays both a horizontal X axis and a vertical Y axis. You can format how these axes appear and how data values are displayed.

To format a specific axis, select either **Horizontal (Category) Axis** or **Vertical (Value) Axis** as the current selection on the Format tab, and click the **Format Selection** button to display the Format Axis panel.

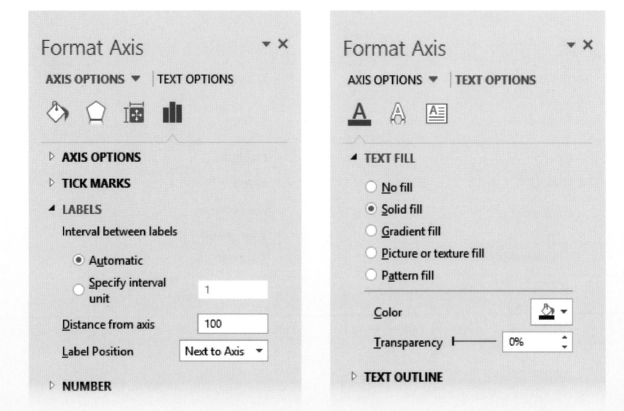

To format nontext elements on the selected axis, select the **Axis Options** tab. From here, click one of the four icons to configure **Fill & Line, Effects, Size & Properties,** or **Axis Options,** respectively. Select **Size & Properties** to configure alignment, text direction, and margins; select **Axis Options** to configure axis type, units, tick marks, labels, and number format.

To format all the text along the selected axis, select the **Text Options** tab. From here, click one of the three icons to configure **Text Fill & Outline, Text Effects,** or **Textbox** options, respectively. For each selected item, scroll down to see all available formatting options. Click an option to apply it to all the text on the axis.

Formatting Axis Titles

If you choose to display titles for a given axis, you can configure how those axis titles appear. Select either **Horizontal (Category) Axis Title** or **Vertical (Value) Axis Title** as the current selection on the Format tab, and click the **Format Selection** button to display the Format Axis Title panel.

To format the area behind the axis title, select the **Title Options** tab. From here, click one of the three icons to configure **Fill & Line**, **Effects**, or **Size & Properties**, respectively.

To format the text of the axis title, select the **Text Options** tab. From here, click one of the three icons to configure **Text Fill & Outline**, **Text Effects**, or **Textbox** options, respectively. For each selected item, scroll down to see all available formatting options. Click an option to apply it to the axis title text.

Formatting the Chart Title

If you choose to display a title for your chart, you can easily format that title by changing its font, font size, color, even background attributes. Select **Chart Title** as the current selection on the Format tab, and click the **Format Selection** button to display the Format Chart Title panel.

Format Chart Title ▾ ✕	Format Chart Title ▾ ✕
TITLE OPTIONS ▾ | TEXT OPTIONS	TITLE OPTIONS ▾ | TEXT OPTIONS
◇ ⬠ 🔧	**A** 𝐀 🄰
◢ ALIGNMENT	▷ TEXT FILL
Vertical alignment [Middle Ce... ▾]	◢ TEXT OUTLINE
Text direction [Horizontal ▾]	⦿ No line
Custom angle [0° ⬍]	○ Solid line
☐ Resize shape to fit text	○ Gradient line
☑ Allow text to overflow shape	
Left margin [0.1" ⬍]	
Right margin [0.1" ⬍]	
Top margin [0.05" ⬍]	
Bottom margin [0.05" ⬍]	

To format the area behind the chart title, select the **Title Options** tab. From here, click one of the three icons to configure **Fill & Line**, **Effects**, or **Size & Properties**, respectively.

To format the title text, select the **Text Options** tab. From here, click one of the three icons to configure **Text Fill & Outline**, **Text Effects**, or **Textbox** options, respectively. For each selected item, scroll down to see all available formatting options. Click an option to apply it to the axis title text.

Formatting Data Labels

If you choose to display data labels, you can format these text labels in a variety of ways. What's more, you format the labels for each data series separately.

To format data labels for a specific data series, select **Series "X" Data Labels** as the current selection on the Format tab, and click the **Format Selection** button to display the Format Data Labels panel.

To format the area behind each label, select the **Label Options** tab. From here, click one of the four icons to configure **Fill & Line**, **Effects**, **Size & Properties**, or **Label Options**, respectively. Select **Size & Properties** to configure label size, alignment, text rotation, and margins; select **Label Options** to configure what type of label is displayed and number format.

To format the data label text, select the **Text Options** tab. From here, click one of the three icons to configure **Text Fill & Outline**, **Text Effects**, or **Textbox** options, respectively. For each selected item, scroll down to see all available formatting options. Click an option to apply it to all the text on the axis.

Formatting a Data Table

If you choose to display a data table beneath your chart, you configure how that table appears in your worksheet. Select **Data Table** as the current selection on the Format tab, and click the **Format Selection** button to display the Format Data Table panel.

Format Data Table ▾ ✕	Format Data Table ▾ ✕
TABLE OPTIONS ▾ | TEXT OPTIONS	TABLE OPTIONS ▾ | TEXT OPTIONS
◊ ⬠ ◧	A A A≡
◢ **DATA TABLE OPTIONS**	▷ **TEXT FILL**
Table Borders	◢ **TEXT OUTLINE**
☑ Horizontal	◉ No line
☑ Vertical	○ Solid line
☑ Outline	○ Gradient line
☑ Show legend keys	

To format the nontext elements of the data table, select the **Table Options** tab. From here, click one of the three icons to configure **Fill & Line**, **Effects**, or **Table Options**, respectively. Click the **Table Options** to configure table borders.

To format the text and numbers in the data table, select the **Text Options** tab. From here, click one of the three icons to configure **Text Fill & Outline**, **Text Effects**, or **Textbox** options, respectively. For each selected item, scroll down to see all available formatting options. Click an option to apply it to the axis title text.

Formatting Gridlines

Most chart types (pie charts being a notable exception) let you display either vertical or horizontal gridlines to help viewers better grasp the values of each data series presented. You can change the size and type of gridline, gridline color, and various visual effects.

To format your chart's gridlines, select **Vertical (Value) Axis Major Gridlines** as the current selection on the Format tab, and click the **Format Selection** button to display the Format Major Gridlines panel.

To format the type, size, and color of your gridlines, click the **Fill & Line** icon.

To apply various visual effects to the gridlines, click the **Effects** icon. From here you can configure shadow, glow, and soft edge effects.

Formatting the Legend

For charts displaying more than one data series (in either column, bar, or line format), a legend helps clarify the data represented. If you've chosen to display a legend, you can easily format its visual appearance, including borders, colors, and text font and size.

To format your chart's legend, select **Legend** as the current selection on the Format tab, and click the **Format Selection** button to display the Format Legend panel.

> 🕐 **Tip**
>
> You can easily move the legend to another location on your chart by selecting the legend with your mouse and dragging it to the new position.

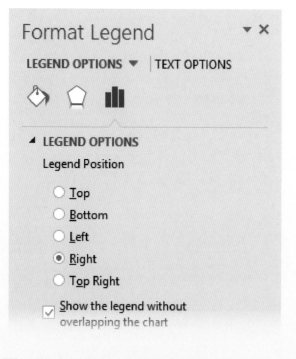

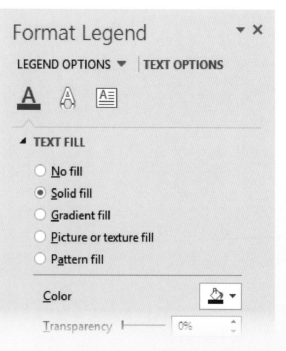

To format the nontext elements of the legend, select the **Legend Options** tab. From here, click one of the three icons to configure **Fill & Line**, **Effects**, or **Legend Options**, respectively. Click the **Legend Options** to configure the position of the legend—Top, Bottom, Left, Right, or Top Right.

To format the text inside the legend, select the **Text Options** tab. From here, click one of the three icons to configure **Text Fill & Outline**, **Text Effects**, or **Textbox** options, respectively. For each selected item, scroll down to see all available formatting options. Click an option to apply it to the axis title text.

Formatting 3-D Rotation

If you've created a 3-D chart of almost any type, you might want to vary the chart's angle, elevation, or perspective to better show the individual data points. You can do this by formatting either the chart area or plot area in the chart.

Display the Format panel, select the **Chart Options** or **Plot Area Options** tab, click the **Effects** icon, and go to the **3-D Rotation** section.

To rotate the chart left or right, use the **X Rotation** control. To rotate the chart up or down, use the **Y Rotation** control. To change the 3-D perspective of the chart, use the **Perspective** control. You can use the up and down arrows on each control or enter precise values for each setting.

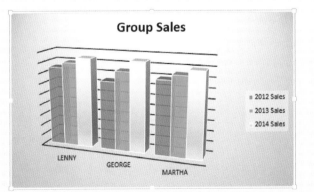

Formatting Data Series

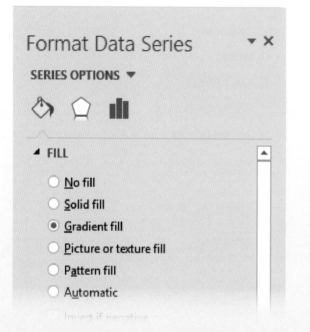

Finally, we come to the meaty part of any chart—the bars, columns, lines, or pie slices that express the values for each data series. You don't have to be content with the color, size, or shape of a data series. You can configure almost every aspect of each series in the chart.

To format the data series in your chart, select **Series "X"** (where "X" is the number of the selected series) as the current selection on the Format tab, and click the **Format Selection** button to display the Format Data Series panel.

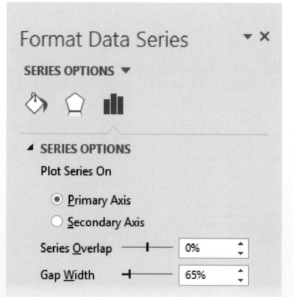

To format the series' fill and line types and colors, click the **Fill & Line** icon. To format the series' shadow, glow, edge, and 3-D effects, click the **Effects** icon.

To format the width and depth of each element, as well as the gap between bars and columns, click the **Series Options** icon. Also select this icon to change the shape of elements in 3-D charts. (For example, instead of displaying traditional rectangular bars and columns, you can display pyramids, cylinders, and cones.)

Formatting a Pie Chart

Pie charts are a little different from row, column, or line charts. Let's look at some of the unique formatting available when you create a pie chart in your worksheet.

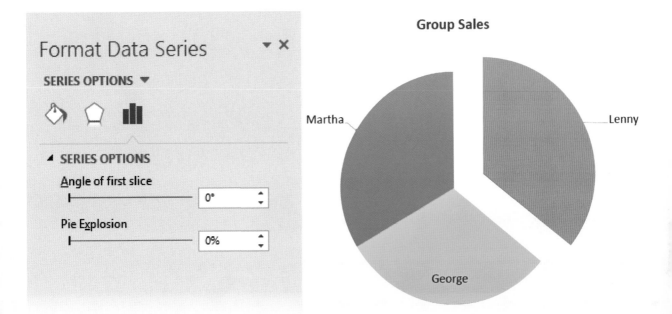

To rotate the chart so the slices are in different positions, display the Format Data Series panel, click the **Series Options** icon, and adjust the **Angle of first slice** control.

To explode the slices of the pie, display the Format Data Series panel, click the **Series Options** icon, and adjust the **Pie Explosion** control. To explode just a single slice, go to the chart itself and use your mouse to click and drag the slice outward. To return to a full pie, click and drag the slice back inward.

 Tip

To format a single bar, column, or pie slice separate from other similar elements in the series, double-click that individual element in the chart. This displays the Format Data Point panel, and you can configure the appropriate settings from here.

Chapter 10

Adding Graphics

When you're prepping a spreadsheet for print or presentation, you might find that simple numbers and charts aren't compelling enough. Sometimes you need to spruce things up, visually, to better engage your audience. Serious number-crunchers might deride this as useless window dressing, but as professional window dressers will attest, you'll attract a lot more attention if you make things a tad prettier.

To that end, Excel enables you to insert all sorts of graphics into a worksheet. You can add photographs, clip art, various "smart" icons, text boxes, and even simple shapes. It's all in service of better telling your story—to put a friendly face on the numbers you need to present.

In This Chapter

- Adding a photograph to a worksheet
- Adding clip art
- Adding SmartArt
- Drawing a shape
- Adding WordArt text
- Adding a text box

Inserting a Photo

When it comes to putting a friendly face on your numerical data, nothing helps more than a literal friendly face—in the form of a photograph. Excel makes it easy to insert any digital photograph you've taken into a worksheet. You can even insert photos you find on the web, which is a great source for stock photography.

To insert a picture stored on your computer or network, place the cursor in the worksheet where you want the picture to appear, and select the **Insert** tab on the Ribbon. Click the **Illustrations** button, and select **Pictures**. When the Insert Pictures dialog box appears, navigate to and select the desired photo, and click the **Insert** button.

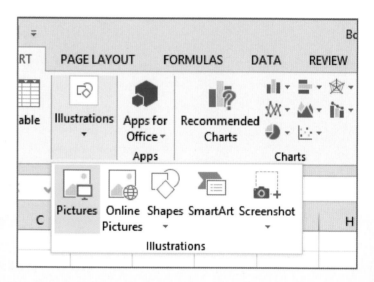

To insert a picture from the web, place the cursor in the worksheet where you want the picture to appear, and click the **Insert** tab. Click the **Illustrations** button, and select **Online Pictures**. When the Insert Pictures pane appears, use Bing Image Search to search for a specific type of picture. When the search results appear, click the image you want to insert, and click the **Insert** button.

resize handle

Once you've inserted a picture, it appears at its full size in your spreadsheet. Resize the picture as necessary by clicking and dragging one of the resize handles at the corner of the image. If you want to move the picture to another location in the worksheet, just use the mouse to drag it there.

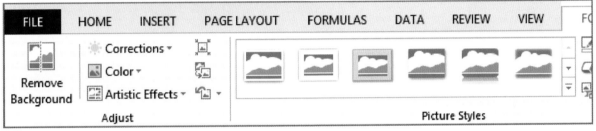

To edit the appearance of the picture, select the **Format** tab, go to the **Adjust** section, and use the **Corrections**, **Color**, and **Artistic Effects** controls accordingly.

Excel offers several predesigned pictures styles that affect the photo's appearance. Select the **Format** tab, go to the **Picture Styles** section, and make a selection.

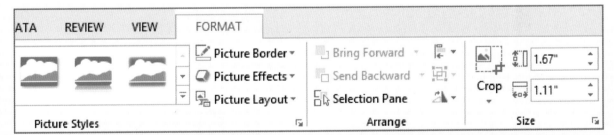

You also can add a border to the picture, as well as apply various picture effects. Select the **Format** tab, go to the **Picture Styles** section, and use the **Picture Border** and **Picture Effects** controls.

Alternatively, select the **Format** tab, go to the **Size** section, and select a new **Height** and **Width** for the picture. You can also use the **Crop** button to crop the picture to its most important elements.

Inserting a Clip Art Image

Microsoft offers a wide selection of clip art online for free at the Office.com website. You can easily insert this clip art into your Excel worksheet to illustrate the data or analysis you're presenting—and then format the clip art to visually match the rest of your presentation.

1 Place the cursor in the worksheet where you want the image to appear, and click the **Insert** tab on the Ribbon, go to the **Illustrations** section, and click the **Online Pictures** button.

2 When the Insert Pictures pane appears, go to the **Office.com Clip Art** section, enter a description of the type of art you're looking for, and press **Enter**.

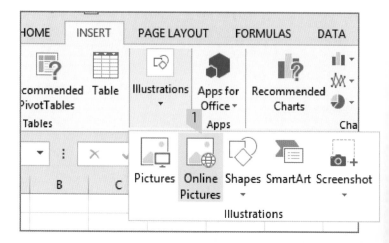

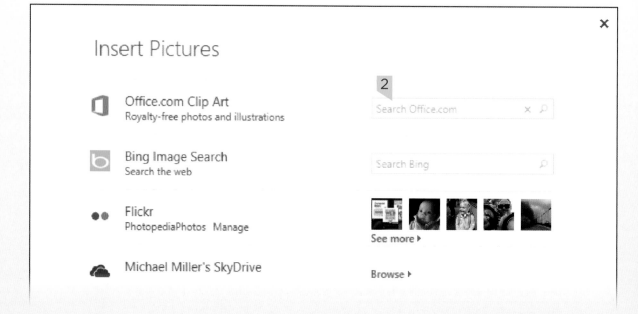

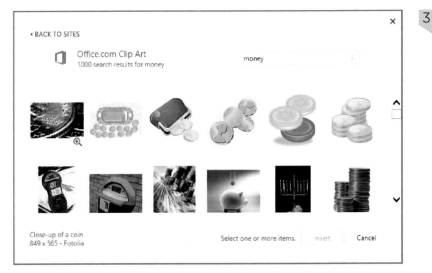

3 You now see clip art images that match your query. Click the image you want to insert, and click the **Insert** button.

resize handle

4 The clip art image is now inserted into your spreadsheet. Resize the art as necessary by clicking and dragging one of the resize handles at the corner of the image. Alternatively, select the **Format** tab, go to the **Size** section, and select a new **Height** and **Width** for the image. You can also use the **Crop** button to crop an image to its most important elements.

5 Use the other controls on the **Format** tab to change the appearance of the clip art. Select a specific style from the **Picture Styles** section, or adjust the appearance of the art in the **Adjust** section. You even can add a border or other picture effects using the appropriate controls on this tab.

Inserting SmartArt

Excel includes a number of predefined "smart" shapes, into you which you can add your own text and images. This so-called SmartArt is a great way to add organization charts, flow charts, pyramid charts, and the like to a worksheet.

1 Place the cursor in the worksheet where you want the SmartArt to appear, and click the **Insert** tab on the Ribbon. Click the **Illustrations** button, and click the **SmartArt** button.

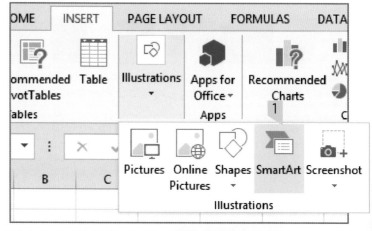

2 When the Choose a SmartArt Graphic dialog box appears, select the type of graphic you want from the list on the left—List, Process, Cycle, Hierarchy, Relationship, Matrix, Pyramid, Picture, or Office.com (online SmartArt). Select the specific art you want, and click the **OK** button.

3 The SmartArt image is now placed on your worksheet. Using your mouse, click in a text placeholder to enter your own text. If the SmartArt lets you include your own images, click an image placeholder to select a photograph or image.

4 In some instances, it might be easier to enter SmartArt text in an outline format. (This approach makes it easier to expand or contract the SmartArt for your specific text.) Select the **Design** tab on the Ribbon, go to the **Create Graphic** section, and click the **Text Pane** button to display a text pane for data entry. Enter your text here.

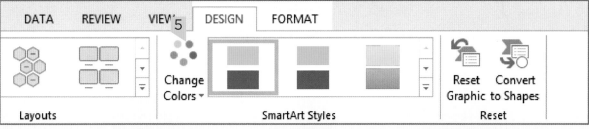

5 To change the color of the selected SmartArt, select the **Design** tab on the Ribbon, go to the **SmartArt Styles** section, click the **Change Colors** button, and select a new color scheme.

6 To change the style of the selected SmartArt, select the **Design** tab on the Ribbon, go to the **SmartArt Styles** section, and select a new style.

Inserting a Shape

SmartArt is useful for presenting certain types of complex information, but sometimes all you need is a simple shape—a line, circle, or arrow. To that end, Excel offers a variety of shapes you can insert anywhere on a worksheet, for whatever effect you have in mind.

1 Select the **Insert** tab on the Ribbon, click the **Illustrations** button, and click **Shapes**.

2 Excel displays the available shapes. Select the specific shape you want to draw.

3 Use your mouse to "draw" the shape onto your spreadsheet. Position the mouse where you want the shape to start, and click and drag the mouse to where you want the shape to end. Release the mouse button to insert the shape you've just drawn.

> **Tip**
>
> You can resize any shape or image by clicking and dragging one of the object's corner handles. You also can rotate most images by grabbing the rotation handle at the top of the object and dragging it clockwise or counterclockwise.

4 To apply a predesigned visual style for the shape, select the **Format** tab, go to the **Shape Styles** section, and select a style.

You can also change the shape's fill color and outline weight and color, and apply various special effects (shadow, reflection, glow, and so forth). Select the **Format** tab, go to the **Shape Styles** section, and use the **Shape Fill**, **Shape Outline**, and **Shape Effects** controls as necessary.

Inserting a Text Box

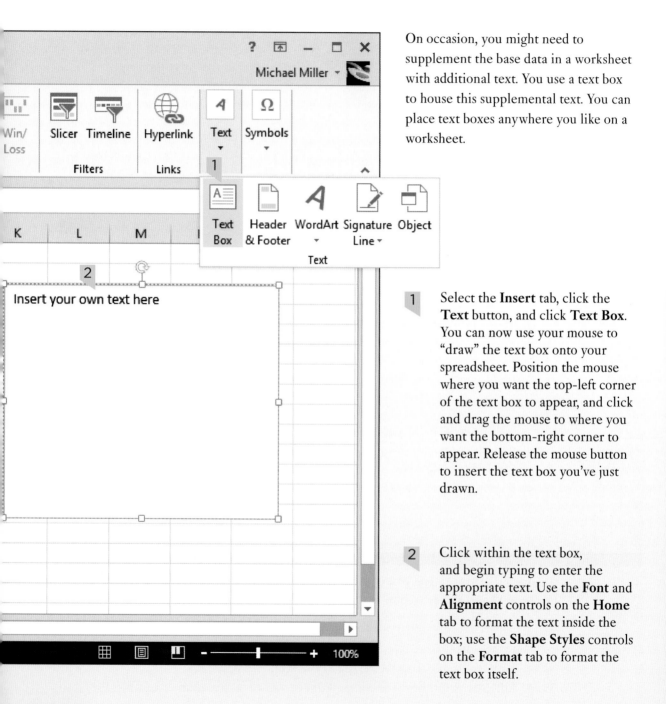

On occasion, you might need to supplement the base data in a worksheet with additional text. You use a text box to house this supplemental text. You can place text boxes anywhere you like on a worksheet.

1 Select the **Insert** tab, click the **Text** button, and click **Text Box**. You can now use your mouse to "draw" the text box onto your spreadsheet. Position the mouse where you want the top-left corner of the text box to appear, and click and drag the mouse to where you want the bottom-right corner to appear. Release the mouse button to insert the text box you've just drawn.

2 Click within the text box, and begin typing to enter the appropriate text. Use the **Font** and **Alignment** controls on the **Home** tab to format the text inside the box; use the **Shape Styles** controls on the **Format** tab to format the text box itself.

Inserting WordArt

Excel also includes a fancier text feature, dubbed WordArt, that treats text as an image, thus enabling you to apply more sophisticated visual effects to the text. Use WordArt when you want to insert a stunning title or comment into a worksheet.

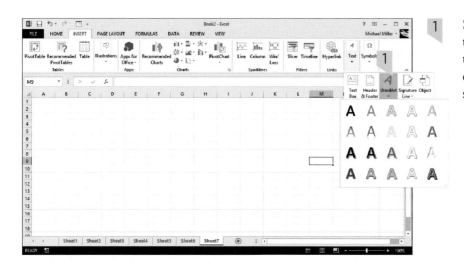

1 Select the **Insert** tab, click the **Text** button, click the **WordArt** button, and choose a particular text style.

2 A WordArt placeholder is inserted into the center of the screen. Use your mouse to reposition and resize it as necessary. Double-click inside the placeholder to type your own text. And use the **WordArt Styles** section to apply predefined visual styles to the text.

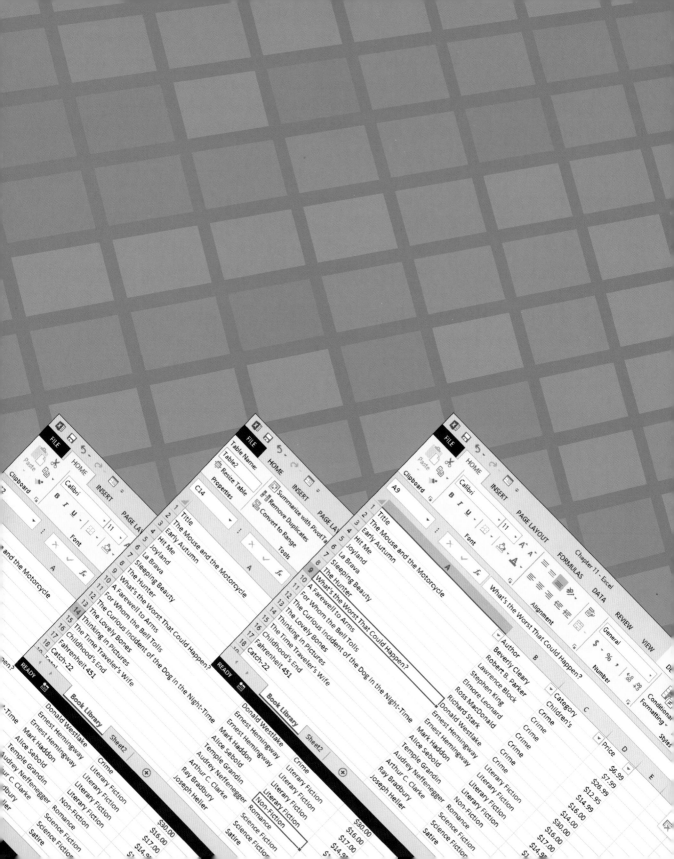

Chapter 11

Working with Tables

Excel is a spreadsheet program, but it can also function as a database. A database differs from a spreadsheet in that it contains distinct data records, each with one or more data fields. To add new data to a database, you simply fill in the appropriate fields.

When you use Excel as a database, you gain new commands and functions that enable you to better organize, manipulate, and analyze your data in ways not possible with a normal Excel spreadsheet. Excel offers database functionality in the form of tables, which are like mini-databases within a worksheet.

Why use an Excel table instead of a traditional spreadsheet? Excel's tables enable you to filter and sort the data in a variety of ways not possible in a normal spreadsheet. You can display only those fields that match a given criteria and in the order you want. And whenever you add new data to the table, the table automatically expands; you don't have to reselect the new range. Finally, any charts referencing the table are also automatically updated when you add new data to the table.

Bottom line, an Excel table is a great way to manage database-like information in a familiar spreadsheet format. Use tables when you want to create a home or work inventory, manage personal records, or catalog specific items.

In This Chapter

- Creating a table from a range of cells
- Adding and deleting records in a table
- Adding and deleting columns in a table
- Sorting and filtering tables
- Displaying totals for table columns
- Turning a table back into a range of cells
- Formatting a table

Converting a Range to a Table

An Excel table is just an extension of a normal Excel worksheet. If you properly plan the construction of a worksheet, it's easy to convert your data into a table—and then access it as you would a database.

When you're planning how to organize your data in a worksheet, use rows for records (one row per record) and columns for fields within each record. For example, if you're inventorying your book collection, each row should be an individual book, with columns for fields such as author, publisher, category, and the like. Be sure the first row of the table range contains the field names.

When you've constructed the format for your data, and maybe even added a few rows of records, you can convert that range of cells into a proper Excel table.

A	B	C	D	E	F
	Title	Author	Category	Price	
	The Hunter	Richard Stark	Crime	$14.00	
	The Curious Incident of the Dog in the Night-Time	Mark Haddon	Literary Fiction	$14.95	
	Joyland	Stephen King	Crime	$12.95	
	Fahrenheit 451	Ray Bradbury	Science Fiction	$13.99	
	Early Autumn	Robert B. Parker	Crime	$7.99	
	A Farewell to Arms	Ernest Hemingway	Literary Fiction	$16.00	
	Childhood's End	Arthur C. Clarke	Science Fiction	$7.99	
	La Brava	Elmore Leonard	Crime	$14.99	
	The Lovely Bones	Alice Sebold	Literary Fiction	$14.99	
	The Time Traveler's Wife	Audrey Neffenegger	Romance	$14.95	
	Catch-22	Joseph Heller	Satire	$16.00	
	For Whom the Bell Tolls	Ernest Hemingway	Literary Fiction	$17.00	
	Hit Me	Lawrence Block	Crime	$26.99	
	Sleeping Beauty	Ross MacDonald	Crime	$16.00	
	Thinking in Pictures	Temple Grandin	Non-Fiction	$15.00	
	What's the Worst That Could Happen?	Donald Westlake	Crime	$30.00	

1 Use your mouse or keyboard to select the range of cells you want to include in your table. The top row of cells in the range must contain the field names.

2 Select the **Home** tab on the Ribbon, go to the **Styles** section, and click the **Format as Table** button. This displays the table styles gallery. Click the visual style you want to apply to your table.

3 When the Format As Table dialog box appears, check the **My table has headers** option, and click **OK**. The selected range is now formatted as a table, complete with pull-down headers (the down arrows next to each header cell).

Format As Table

Where is the data for your table?

=$B$1:$E$17

☑ My table has headers

OK   Cancel

Adding New Data to a Table

A database table is a living thing; you're always adding more records to it. For example, if you construct a table for your home inventory, you'll want to add new records for each new major purchase you make.

Excel enables you to add new data to a table in two ways. You can simply insert new rows into the worksheet itself, or you can use a data form to insert information about each new record you add. The latter approach should be more familiar to you if you're used to working with conventional databases, and it can be faster for inputting multiple records.

If you're not used to using forms to enter data, don't fret; a data form is nothing more than an Excel dialog box that displays the fields of a database. Each record is shown in a separate page in the dialog box, and you can easily switch from record to record and add new records to the table.

Unfortunately, for some reason, Excel hides the button you need to use to display and use data forms. You can, however, add a Form button to Excel's Quick Access Toolbar, which is useful if you work with a lot of tables.

To add a new record directly to the worksheet, begin typing in the row directly below the last row of the table. The selected range of the table automatically expands to include the new row in the table. (Don't worry about inserting the new row in a certain order. The row will appear in the right place when you later sort the table data.)

4	Joyland	Stephen King	Crime
5	La Brava	Elmore Leonard	Crime
6	Sleeping Beauty	Ross MacDonald	Crime
7	The Hunter	Richard Stark	Crime
8	What's the Worst That Could Happen?	Donald Westlake	Crime
9	A Farewell to Arms	Ernest Hemingway	Literary Fiction
10	For Whom the Bell Tolls	Ernest Hemingway	Literary Fiction
11	The Curious Incident of the Dog in the Night-Time	Mark Haddon	Literary Fiction
12	The Lovely Bones	Alice Sebold	Literary Fiction
13	Thinking in Pictures	Temple Grandin	Non-Fiction
14	The Time Traveler's Wife	Audrey Neffenegger	Romance
15	Catch-22	Joseph Heller	Satire
18	The Mouse and the Motorcycle	Beverly Cleary	Children's
19	Little Green		
20			

Book Library   Sheet2   ⊕

READY   FILTER MODE

🕐 Tip

To display the Form button, click the down-arrow at the right side of the Quick Access Toolbar and select **More Commands…**. When the Excel Options dialog box appears, pull down the **Choose commands from** list and select **All Commands**. Select **Form…** in the left column, and click the **Add** button. Click **OK** when you're done, and the Form button now appears on the Quick Access Toolbar.

| FILE | HOME | INSERT | PAGE LAYOUT |

Calibri   11   A A

Paste   B I U ▾ ▾ ▾ A ▾

Clipboard   Font

B19   ✕ ✓ fx

Book Library   ? ✕

Title:
Author:
Category:
Price:

2 New Record
New
Delete
Restore
Find Prev
Find Next
Criteria
Close

1 To add a new record using a form, position the cursor anywhere within the current table, and click the **Form…** button on the Quick Access Toolbar.

2 When the form dialog box appears, click the **New** button.

3 Enter data for each of the fields in the new record. Click **New** to add another record or **Close** when you're done entering data. The new record is automatically added to the end of the table.

Removing Rows from a Table

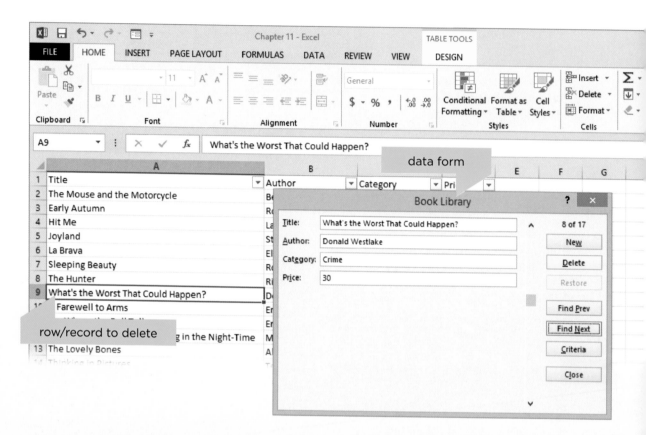

Each row in a table represents a single record within the underlying database. How, then, do you delete records from the database? For example, you've built a database table to catalog your book collection. At some point, you might sell or lose a given book and want to remove that book from your inventory by deleting that book's record from the database.

Deleting a record is as simple as deleting a row from the table. You can delete rows directly from the worksheet or by using the table's data form dialog box.

To delete a row directly from the worksheet, position the cursor anywhere in that row. Select the **Home** tab on the Ribbon, go to the **Cells** section, click the **Delete** button, and select **Delete Table Rows**.

1. To delete a record using a form, position the cursor anywhere within the current table and click the **Form…** button on the Quick Access Toolbar.

2. When the form dialog box appears, click the **Find Prev** and **Find Next** buttons until the record you want to delete is displayed.

3. Click the **Delete** button. This record is automatically deleted from the table.

Inserting Table Columns

As you've learned, to add a new row to a data table, you need only enter data into the first blank row underneath the current table, and the table expands to contain the new row. You also can add new columns to a table to contain additional fields of information you've decided to include in your database.

When you insert a new column into a table, you essentially add a new field to each record or row in the table. When you do this, you need to return to all the existing records and enter information for the new field.

1 Position the cursor anywhere within the column to the *right* of where you want the new column to appear.

2 Select the **Home** tab on the Ribbon, go to the **Cells** section, click the **Insert** button, and select **Insert Table Columns to the Left**. The new column is inserted into the table. You need to edit the column header with the proper field name.

> 🕐 **Tip**
>
> To add a new column to the end (the far right) of a table, position the cursor in the current far right column, click the **Insert** button, and select **Insert Table Columns to the Right**.

Deleting Table Columns

Just as you can insert new columns (fields) into a table, you also can delete existing columns. When you delete a table column, you essentially remove the associated field from each record (row) in the table.

1. Position the cursor anywhere within the column you want to delete.

2. Select the **Home** tab on the Ribbon, go to the **Cells** section, click the **Delete** button, and select **Delete Table Columns**. The selected column is deleted from the table.

Sorting a Table

One of the benefits of using a table to store data in a worksheet is the ease with which you can sort that data. In effect, you use Excel's Sort command to display your database records in whatever order you want, based on the fields within the database.

1 Click the down-arrow next the header for the column/field by which you want to sort.

2 To sort the data in alphabetic order, click **Sort A to Z**. To sort in reverse alphabetic order, click **Sort Z to A**. (If you're sorting numeric data, select either **Sort Smallest to Largest** or **Sort Largest to Smallest**.) The rows in the table are now sorted by the column you selected.

Filtering Data in a Table

You might not want to display every record in your database table. For example, if you've built a table for your book collection, at some point, you might only want to see those books in a given genre or by a specific author.

In this instance, you want Excel to filter the data in the table to display only those records that meet a given criteria—typically a specific value or range of values for a given field/column. It's easy to do.

1 Click the down-arrow next to the header for the column/field you want to use for the filter.

2 By default, all the values entered for this field are checked. Uncheck those values you *don't* want to display; leave checked those values you want to display. To redisplay all the records in your table, check the **Select All** option.

Adding Column Totals

If you have a field or column in your table that contains numeric data—the value of items in a household inventory, for example—you might want to include a total of those values. Excel enables you to easily add column totals to a table.

1 Select the **Design** tab, go to the **Table Style Options** section, and check the **Total Row** option.

					Chapter 11 - Excel					TABLE TOOLS

JT   FORMULAS   DATA   REVIEW   VIEW   DESIGN

Insert Slicer   Export   Refresh

1 ☑ Header Row   ☐ First Column
   ☑ Total Row   ☐ Last Column
   ☐ Banded Rows   ☐ Banded Columns

External Table Data   Table Style Options

tephen King

2 This adds a *Total* row to the bottom of the table. Position the cursor in the **Total** row cell for the column you want to total, click the down-arrow, and select **Sum**. The Total row now contains a value for the sum of the selected column.

	Category ▼	Price ▼	E	F
emingway	Literary Fiction	$16.00		
emingway	Literary Fiction	$17.00		
ddon	Literary Fiction	$14.95		
old	Literary Fiction	$14.99		
Grandin	Non-Fiction	$15.00		
Neffenegger	Romance	$14.95		
. Clarke	Science Fiction	$7.99		
bury	Science Fiction	$13.99		
Heller	Satire	$16.00		
		$260.78 ▼		

None
Average
Count
Count Numbers
Max
Min
Sum
StdDev
Var
More Functions..

🕐 **Tip**

The SUM function isn't the only option available in the Total row. When you click the down-arrow in a Total cell, you can opt to use the AVERAGE, COUNT (count cells with numbers), COUNTA (count nonempty cells), MIN, STDDEV, or VAR functions—or, if you click **More Functions...**, any applicable Excel function.

Converting a Table to a Range

There might come a time when you no longer want to work with your table as a database. At any time, you can convert an Excel table to a standard range of cells. (Note, however, that converting a table to a range does not revert to the original formatting for that range.)

10	Title	Author	Category	Price
10	A Farewell to Arms	Ernest Hemingway	Literary Fiction	$16.
11	For Whom the Bell Tolls	Ernest Hemingway	Literary Fiction	$17.
12	The Curious Incident of the Dog in the Night-Time	Mark Haddon	Literary Fiction	$14.
13	The Lovely Bones	Alice Sebold	Literary Fiction	$14.
14	Thinking in Pictures	Temple Grandin	Non-Fiction	$15.
15	The Time Traveler's Wife	Audrey Neffenegger	Romance	$14.
16	Childhood's End	Arthur C. Clarke	Science Fiction	$7.
17	Fahrenheit 451	Ray Bradbury	Science Fiction	$13.
18	Catch-22	Joseph Heller	Satire	$16.
19	Total			$260.

1   Select any cell in the table.

2   Select the **Design** tab, go to the **Tools** section, and click the **Convert to Range** button. When prompted to confirm the change, click **Yes**.

Applying Table Styles

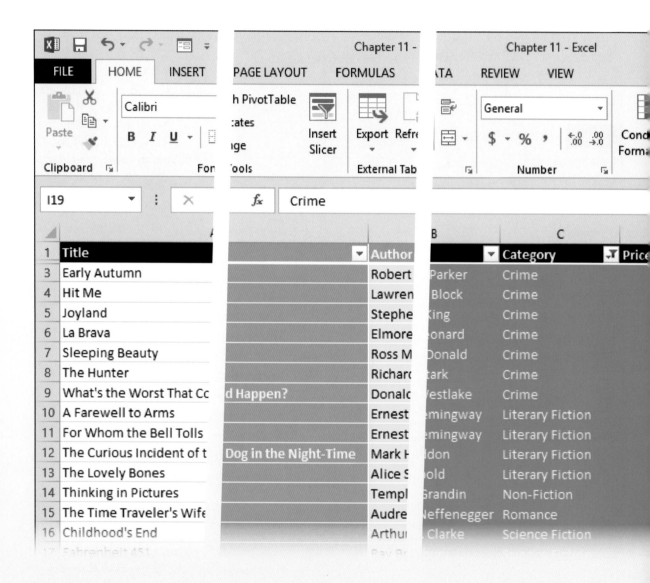

Excel lets you format your tables in any number of ways. You can bold the first or last column in the table, display shaded (banded) rows or columns, or choose from a variety of colorful built-in table styles.

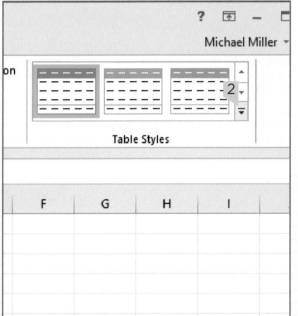

1 Select the **Design** tab, and go to the **Table Style Options** section. To hide the header row, uncheck **Header Row**. To display banded rows (shading every other row), check **Banded Rows**. To display banded columns (shading every other column), check **Banded Columns**. To bold the first column (highlighting the first field in the database), check **First Column**. To bold the last column, check **Last Column**. To hide the down-arrows for each row header, uncheck **Filter Button**.

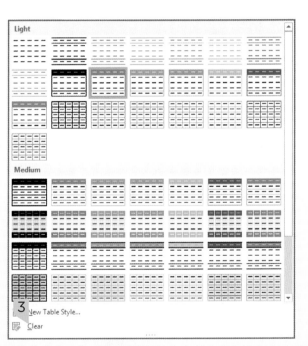

2 To apply a new table style, click the down scroll arrow in the **Table Styles** section of the **Design** tab.

3 Click the table style you want to apply. To remove all formatting from the table, click **Clear** at the bottom.

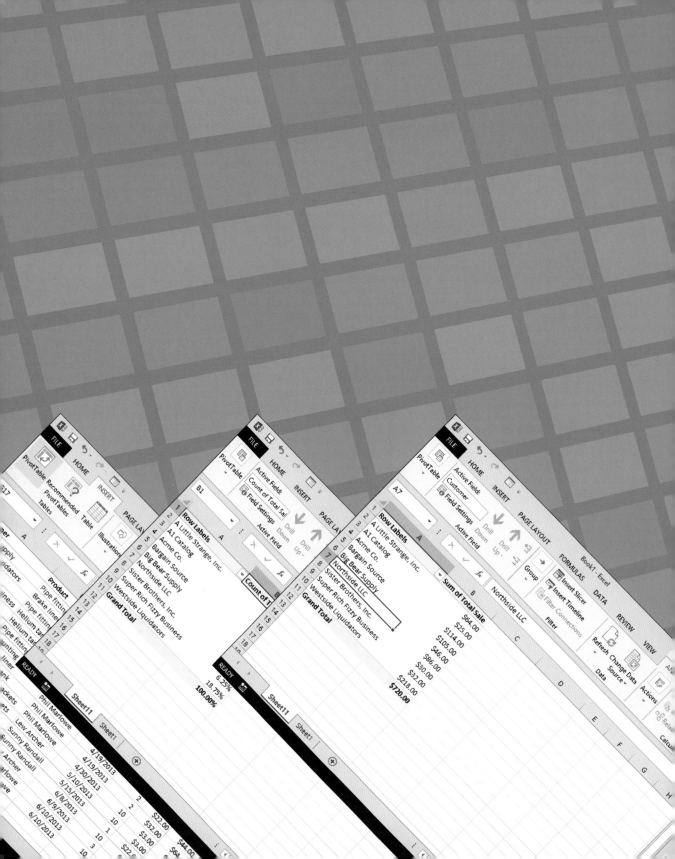

Chapter 12

Working with PivotTables

You can store a lot of data in an Excel spreadsheet. Sometimes, however, there's just too much data to easily analyze in the traditional row-and-column format.

When you have multiple variables in multiple records, you can make your data more manageable by using Excel's PivotTables feature. A PivotTable lets you manipulate complex data in various ways and then summarizes the results.

In essence, a PivotTable is an interactive table that contains large amounts of data. You can rotate the rows and columns of the PivotTable to view your data in different ways as well as sort and filter the contents to provide different "cuts" of the information.

As such, the PivotTable tool is one of the most powerful features of Excel. With a PivotTable, your data isn't static; you can easily change the way it's presented and summarized with just a few clicks of the mouse.

You should create a PivotTable when you have large amounts of data with multiple columns or fields, and when you want to analyze related totals from different columns. A PivotTable is especially useful when you want to compare multiple variables for each record in a worksheet database.

In This Chapter

- Understanding PivotTables
- Building PivotTables
- Inserting PivotTable fields
- Calculating different values
- Editing the PivotTable's source data
- Sorting and filtering data in PivotTables
- Displaying data visually with a PivotChart

How PivotTables Work

A PivotTable is a type of interactive table that enables you to sort, filter, combine, and compare large amounts of data. In its power lies the ability to rotate rows and columns to view different summaries of the source data.

Creating a PivotTable

When you create a PivotTable, you take data from one worksheet and insert it, in a different format, in another sheet in the same workbook. You can then use the PivotTable controls to manipulate the way the data is displayed and summarized. This leads to more customized and detailed analysis of the source data—and a better understanding of what's really going on.

The data you use to create a PivotTable must be in its raw format. That is, it shouldn't already be totaled and subtotaled; you'll use the PivotTable tool to do that. A basic list or database table works best, with individual records in each row and data fields in different columns.

If you've already created an Excel data for your table, you can convert it for PivotTable use easily. You also can import data from a Microsoft Access or MS-SQL Server database. The data can be as simple as a one-column list or as complex as you can devise, using multiple columns for each row of data.

	A	B	C
1	**Customer**	**Product**	**Salesperson**
2	Big Bear Supply	Pipe fittings	Lew Archer
3	Westside Liquidators	Brake liner	Lew Archer
4	Acme Co.	Pipe fittings	Phil Marlowe
5	Super Rich Fizzy Business	Helium tank	Lew Archer
6	A Little Strange, Inc.	Helium tank	Sunny Randall
7	Northside LLC	Pipe fittings	Lew Archer
8	Sister Brothers, Inc.	Mounting brackets	Sunny Randall
9	Westside Liquidators	Brake liner	Phil Marlowe
10	Westside Liquidators	Helium tank	Phil Marlowe
11	Acme Co.	Mounting brackets	Phil Marlowe
12	Big Bear Supply	Mounting brackets	Lew Archer
13	Northside LLC	Brake liner	Sunny Randall
14	Acme Co.	Mounting brackets	Sunny Randall
15	Bargain Source	Helium tank	Lew Archer

Reconfiguring a PivotTable

When you build a PivotTable, you're asked which fields (columns) in the original data to include in the PivotTable report. You can display as many or as few columns as you need.

You can then reconfigure the PivotTable to look at your data from just about any angle. You can group multiple columns to view subtotals based on those columns. You can filter the data based on field values. You even can swap rows and columns to create a totally different view of your data.

Customizing Your PivotTable Display

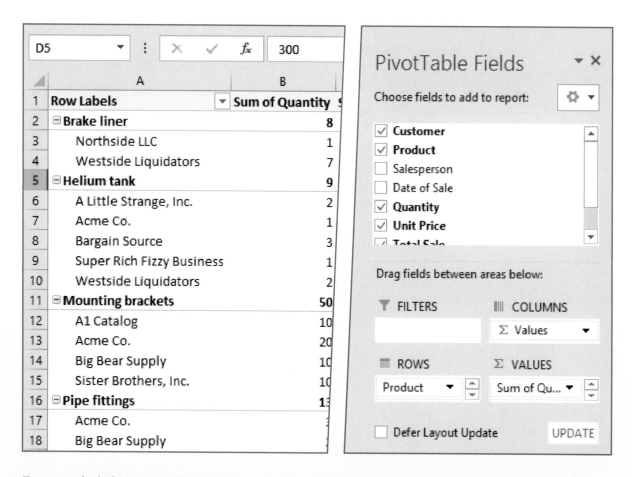

For example, let's say your PivotTable is comprised of rows for each of your company's customers and columns for date of purchase, type of product purchased, amount of purchase, and salesperson for that transaction. Within the PivotTable, you can opt to show and total only those sales by a particular salesperson, only those sales in a given date range, or only those sales of a particular type of product. You can display sales of a given product by a given salesperson, sales to a particular customer in a given date range, and so forth. You can display a summary of dollar sales by salesperson, by month, or by product type. You even can perform other calculations on the data to figure the average dollar sale for each product line or the total number of transactions for each salesperson. The options are almost endless.

	A	B
	A1 ▾ ⋮ ✕ ✓ *fx*	Row Labels
1	**Row Labels** ↓↑	**Sum of Total Sale**
2	⊟ **Lew Archer**	**49.6%**
3	Brake liner	15.3%
4	Helium tank	19.0%
5	Mounting brackets	4.2%
6	Pipe fittings	11.1%
7	⊟ **Phil Marlowe**	**30.8%**
8	Brake liner	6.1%
9	Helium tank	13.8%
10	Mounting brackets	7.6%
11	Pipe fittings	3.3%
12	⊟ **Sunny Randall**	**19.6%**
13	Brake liner	3.1%
14	Helium tank	8.9%
15	Mounting brackets	7.6%
16	**Grand Total**	**100.0%**
17		
18		

PivotTable Fields ▾ ✕

Choose fields to add to report: ⚙ ▾

☐ Customer
☑ **Product**
☑ **Salesperson**
☐ Date of Sale
☐ Quantity
☐ Unit Price
☑ Total Sale

Drag fields between areas below:

▼ FILTERS

▥ COLUMNS

▤ ROWS
Salesperson ▾

Σ VALUES
Sum of Total ... ▾

☐ Defer Layout Update

UPDATE

It's a matter of including the appropriate source data, organized in the right way, and then deciding what questions you want answered. When you ask the questions "How many transactions did Lew Archer make in May?" or "What customers purchased mounting brackets?" or "What was the dollar volume for each salesperson?" the PivotTable is quickly rearranged and recalculated to present the answers as clearly as possible. Excel does all the work, not you.

Creating a PivotTable

You can create a PivotTable from just about any Excel worksheet or external database. We examine how to create a PivotTable from a range of cells, but the other methods take a similar approach.

There are two ways to create a PivotTable. We look at the easiest way first, using Excel's Recommended PivotTables command.

Creating a PivotTable the Easy Way

Start with a range of cells in basic list format. Think of each row as a record in a database and each column as a data field. It helps if each column has a header. You also want to remove any totals or subtotals from the source data. It doesn't matter how the source data is sorted; the PivotTable tool lets you re-sort the data as you like.

> **Note**
>
> To create a PivotTable based on external data from Access or another program, you first have to import that data into your workbook. Select the **Data** tab on the ribbon, go to the **Get External Data** section, and click the appropriate button—**From Access**, **From Web**, **From Text**, or **From Other Sources**. Follow the on-screen instructions to import the selected data.

10	$3.00	$30.00
10	$3.00	$30.00
1	$22.00	$22.00
10	$2.50	$25.00
3	$35.00	$105.00
10	$2.50	1 $25.00
1	$35.00	$35.00

1 Position the cursor in any cell within the range you want to convert to a data table. You don't have to select the entire range (although you can, if you want); Excel determines the source range automatically.

2 Click the **Insert** tab, go to the **Tables** section, and click the **Recommended PivotTables** button.

3 Recommended PivotTables

Sum of Quantity by Product

Row Labels	Sum of Quantity
Brake liner	8
Helium tank	9
Mounting brackets	50
Pipe fittings	13
Grand Total	80

Sum of Unit Price by Sa...

Row Labels	Sum of Unit Price
Lew Archer	108
Phil Marlowe	102.5
Sunny Randall	59.5
Grand Total	270

Sum of Total Sale, Sum ...

Row Labels	Sum of Total Sale	Sum of Unit Price
Lew Archer	357	108
Phil Marlowe	222	102.5
Sunny Randall	141	59.5
Grand Total	720	270

Sum of Unit Price and S...

Sum of Quantity by Product

Row Labels	Sum of Quantity
Brake liner	8
Helium tank	9
Mounting brackets	50
Pipe fittings	13
Grand Total	**80**

Blank PivotTable   Change Source Data...   OK   Cancel

3 The Recommended PivotTables dialog box displays a selection of PivotTables that best match the data you've selected. Click a PivotTable in the left-hand preview pane to see how it looks with your data. Click **OK** to create a PivotTable on a new worksheet in your workbook.

Creating a PivotTable Manually

For most purposes, the Recommended PivotTables function does a good job of creating a basic PivotTable from your selected data. And of course, you can reconfigure, filter, and sort the PivotTable as necessary to create the desired results.

You also can create a PivotTable manually, which may enable you to create the results you want more immediately. You can use this method to import data from an outside source, too, or place the PivotTable on the same worksheet as the source data.

1 Position the cursor in any single cell within the range you want to convert to a PivotTable. You don't have to select the entire range of cells—although you can, if you want.

2 Select the **Insert** tab on the Ribbon, go to the **Tables** section, and click the **PivotTable** button.

Create PivotTable dialog box

3 oose the data that you want to analyze

- ● Select a table or range
  - Table/Range: Sheet1!$A$1:$G$17
- ○ Use an external data source
  - Choose Connection...
  - Connection name:

4 oose where you want the PivotTable report to be placed

- ● New Worksheet
- ○ Existing Worksheet
  - Location:

Choose whether you want to analyze multiple tables

- ☐ Add this data to the Data Model

OK   Cancel

PivotTable Fields ▾ ✕

Choose fields to add to report: ⚙ ▾

5
- ☐ Customer
- ☐ Product
- ☐ Salesperson
- ☐ Date of Sale
- ☐ Quantity
- ☐ Unit Price
- ☐ Total Sale

Drag fields between areas below:

▼ FILTERS   ▥ COLUMNS

≡ ROWS   **6** VALUES

☐ Defer Layout Update   UPDATE

3 Excel now displays the Create PivotTable dialog box. Be sure **Select a table or range** is selected and the correct range is listed in the **Table/Range** box. If not, return to the source worksheet and select the proper range.

4 If you want the PivotTable displayed on a new worksheet, leave the **New Worksheet** option checked. If you prefer to display the PivotTable next to the source data, check **Existing Worksheet**, pull down the **Location** list, and select that worksheet. Click **OK** to create the PivotTable.

> **✎ Note**
>
> If you want to create a PivotTable from an Access database or other external file, click the **PivotTable** button on the **Insert** tab to display the Create PivotTable dialog box. Check the **Use an external data source** option, click the **Choose Connection...** button, and select the external file. Click **OK** when you're done.

5 Excel now displays the PivotTable Fields pane. Check those fields you want to include in the report. As you select fields, Excel builds the PivotTable in the main part of the worksheet.

6 To add a column of values to the PivotTable (along with either a count or total of those values), drag a field from the fields list onto the **Values** box at the bottom of the PivotTable Fields pane.

Adding Fields to a PivotTable

When you want to view or summarize specific data, you need to add the field that contains that data to your PivotTable. A field is essentially a column from your source data. All selected columns are stored in your PivotTable, and you select which ones are displayed and used at any given time.

Fields that contain text data are displayed in the Rows area of the PivotTable—the first column in the PivotTable. If you select multiple text fields, they're listed in the same column, in hierarchical order based on which fields you selected first. To collapse a field level, click the – button next to that field; to expand a collapsed field level, click the + button.

Fields that contain numerical data are typically displayed in the Values area of the PivotTable—columns adjacent to the Rows area. Excel then performs the appropriate mathematical operation on this field data, typically totaling the data with the SUM function.

	Rows area	values column	
1	**Row Labels**	**Sum of Total Sale**	
2	⊟ **Brake liner**	$176.00	
	Lew Archer	$110.00	
	fields in the Rows area	$44.00	
5	Sunny Randall	$22.00	
6	⊟ **Helium tank**	$300.00	
7	Lew Archer	$137.00	
8	Phil Marlowe	$99.00	
9	Sunny Randall	$64.00	
10	⊟ **Mounting brackets**	$140.00	
11	Lew Archer	$30.00	
12	Phil Marlowe	$55.00	
13	Sunny Randall	$55.00	
14	⊟ **Pipe fittings**	$104.00	
15	Lew Archer	$80.00	
16	Phil Marlowe	$24.00	
17	**Grand Total**	$720.00	

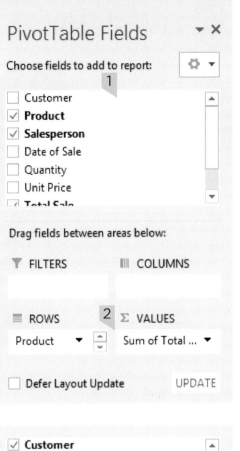

1 Click within the PivotTable to display the PivotTable Fields pane. In the **Choose fields to add to report** section, check those fields you want to appear.

2 To add a field to a specific area (Rows or Values), use your mouse to drag and drop fields from the field list onto the Rows or Values drop zones at the bottom of the PivotTable Fields pane. This method enables you to position numeric fields in the Rows area (first column) or non-numeric fields in the Values columns. Note that all the fields you drop onto the Rows box appear in the first column of the PivotTable, in the order you dropped them. If you drop multiple fields onto the Value box, you create separate columns for each field. (Fields dropped on the Value box are either totaled or counted—via the SUM and COUNT functions—for each Row value.)

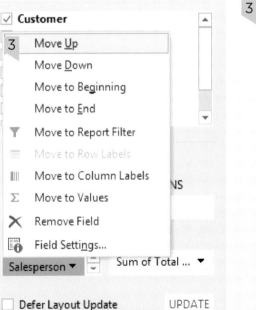

3 The order in which you check or drag a field determines its position in the Rows hierarchy—that is, how the information is arranged. The first field you check is the top-most field in the Rows area, the second field you check appears next, and so on. If you don't like the order in which your field data appears, go to the **Rows** box in the PivotTable Fields pane, click the field you want to reposition, and click either **Move Up** or **Move Down** from the pop-up menu.

Changing Value Calculations

A	B	A	B	B
▾ Labels	▾ Sum of Total Sale	bels ▾	Count of Total Sale	▾ Sum of Total Sale
ttle Strange, Inc.	$64.00	trange, Inc.	6.25%	$64.00
Catalog	$25.00		6.25%	$25.00
ie Co.	$114.00		25.00%	$114.00
gain Source	$105.00		6.25%	$105.00
Bear Supply	$46.00	ply	12.50%	$46.00
thside LLC	$86.00	LLC	12.50%	$86.00
er Brothers, Inc.	$30.00	thers, Inc.	6.25%	$30.00
er Rich Fizzy Business	$32.00	ich Fizzy Business	6.25%	$32.00
stside Liquidators	$218.00	side Liquidators	18.75%	$218.00
nd Total	$720.0	nd Total	100.00%	$720.00

By default, Excel performs the most appropriate mathematical calculation on the fields in the Values columns of the PivotTable. So if you have a field for price, Excel totals the values in that column using the SUM function. If you have a non-numeric field, such as product name, Excel counts the items in that column using the COUNT function.

You can, however, instruct Excel to perform different calculations on any individual Values column. So if you'd rather average the data, you can. Excel also enables you to change what's displayed in the Values column—such as a given field's percentage of the grand total for that column.

1. Select any cell within the Values column you want to change, and select the **Analyze** tab on the Ribbon, go to the **Active Field** section, and click the **Field Settings** button to display the Value Field Settings dialog box.

2. Select the **Summarize Values By** tab, and choose a function from the list.

3. To change what values are displayed in the column rows, select the **Show Values As** tab, and choose an option from the list. For example, you can display values as a percent of the grand total or as a percent of the running total. Click **OK** when you're done.

Changing the Source Data

You can add more data to a PivotTable easily, simply by inserting new rows or columns into the source data in your workbook. When you add new columns to the source data, those new fields appear in the field list for the PivotTable.

1. Return to the worksheet that holds the PivotTable's source data, and insert new rows or columns as appropriate. Move to and select the PivotTable, select the **Analyze** tab, go to the **Data** section, click the **Change Data Source** button, and select **Change Data Source**. This displays the Change PivotTable Data Source dialog box. Be sure the complete range of source data is selected, and click the **OK** button.

2. You now need to refresh the PivotTable to recognize any added fields. Select the **Analyze** tab, go to the **Data** section, and click the **Refresh** button. Any new fields should now appear in the PivotTable Fields pane.

Sorting a PivotTable

Just as you can sort a standard database table by the various field columns, you can also sort a PivotTable by any field in the Rows area of the table.

To sort by one of the lower-hierarchy fields, click the down-arrow next to the **Rows Labels** heading and select **More Sort Options…** to display the Sort (*Category*) dialog box. Check either the **Ascending (A to Z) by** or **Descending (Z to A) by** options, and select a field from the pull-down list. Click **OK** to sort the data.

To sort by the top field in the Rows area, click the down-arrow next to the **Rows Labels** heading, and select either **Sort A to Z** or **Sort Z to A**.

Filtering PivotTable Data with Slicers

When you want to focus on a subset of your data for closer analysis, or just display records that meet specific criteria, you can filter the data in your PivotTable. Excel 2013 offers several different ways to do this.

The easiest way to filter PivotTable data is by creating *slicers* that let you filter data by specific values within a field. You can create slicers for each field in your PivotTable; a slicer has buttons you can click to select or deselect specific values.

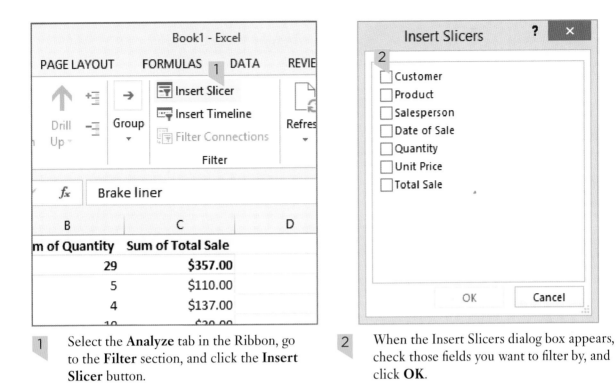

1   Select the **Analyze** tab in the Ribbon, go to the **Filter** section, and click the **Insert Slicer** button.

2   When the Insert Slicers dialog box appears, check those fields you want to filter by, and click **OK**.

3   Excel now creates and displays a slicer for each field you selected. The slicer contains buttons for each value within that field. By default, all the buttons are selected, so all values are displayed. To filter the data to display only those records with a specific value, click to select that specific button. To filter the data by more than one value, press the **Ctrl** button on your keyboard while you click each button.

4   To unfilter the data and display all values again, click the **Clear Filter** button at the top-right corner of the slicer.

Filtering by Date with Timelines

⊿	A	B
1	**Row Labels** ⤓	**Sum of Total Sale**
2	⊟ **A1 Catalog**	**$25.00**
3	6/10/2013	$25.00
4	⊟ **Acme Co.**	**$60.00**
5	6/8/2013	$25.00
6	6/10/2013	$35.00
7	⊟ **Bargain Source**	**$105.00**
8	6/9/2013	$105.00
9	⊟ **Big Bear Supply**	**$30.00**
10	5/10/2013	$30.00
11	⊟ **Northside LLC**	**$22.00**
12	5/15/2013	$22.00
13	**Grand Total**	**$242.00**

timeline control

click to select time periods

Date of Sale

May - Sep 2013   MONTHS ▾

2013

PR   MAY   JUN   JUL   AUG   SEP   OCT

◀   ▶

slider

If one or more of the fields in your PivotTable contain dates, you might want to filter your table to display only those records in a specific date range. You could use a slicer to select specific dates, but that's awkward at best. It's better to specify a date range and, thus, automatically select those records that fall within the range.

Excel 2013 offers a new *timeline* feature for filtering PivotTables by date. When you add a timeline control to your PivotTable, selecting the starting and ending dates to filter is as easy as dragging a slider.

1 Select the **Analyze** tab in the Ribbon, go to the **Filter** section, and click the **Insert Timeline** button.

2 When the Insert Timelines dialog box appears, check those date fields you want to filter by, and click **OK**.

3 Excel now creates and displays a timeline for each date field you selected. To narrow the date range selected, scroll to either end of the timeline and use your mouse to drag the end of the slider to a new date.

4 To change what time periods are displayed, click the down-arrow at the top-right corner of the timeline, and select **Years**, **Quarters**, **Months**, or **Days**.

5 To clear the filter (and display all dates in the PivotTable), click the Clear Filter button.

Other Ways to Filter PivotTable Data

Slicers and timelines make it easy to filter the data in a PivotTable, but you can narrow down what's displayed in several other ways, too. You can filter your data by the primary field, by any field, or by specific criteria, such as greater than or less than. You also can opt to display just the top or bottom five or ten items in the PivotTable.

To filter by the major field in the Rows area, click the down-arrow next to the **Rows Labels** header to display the menu of options. Uncheck those field values you do not want displayed, and click **OK**.

To create a field filter within the PivotTable, go to the PivotTable Fields pane and drag the desired field from the top list to the **Filters** box. This adds a filter header above the PivotTable labeled *Category*. Click the down-arrow next to that header to display the available field values; click a value to display only matching records. (To select more than one value, check the **Select Multiple Items** box first.) Click **OK** to filter the data by the selected values.

To display only those values that meet a specific criteria, click the down-arrow next to the **Rows Labels** header, and select either **Label Filters**, **Value Filters**, or **Date Filters**, depending on the type of data. Select the desired operator, such as Equals…, Does Not Equal…, Begins With…, Contains…, Greater Than…, or Less Than…. This displays a Label Filter, Value Filter, or Date Filter dialog box. Enter a value for the operator into the right text box, and click **OK**.

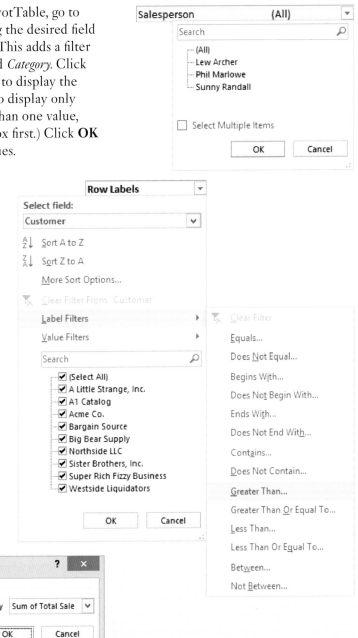

To show the top or bottom items in the PivotTable, click the down-arrow next to the **Rows Labels** header, select **Value Filters**, and click **Top 10**. This displays the Top 10 Filter dialog box. Pull down the first list, and select either **Top** or **Bottom**. Pull down the second list, and select how many items to display. Pull down the third list, and select either **Items**, **Percent**, or **Sum**. Then pull down the final list, and select how you want the data presented. Click **OK** when you're done.

Creating a PivotChart

Excel also lets you create PivotCharts—interactive charts based on PivotTable data. A quick click of the mouse, and the chart changes to reflect the selected data view.

A PivotChart doesn't display all the data in a PivotTable, of course. Typically, a PivotChart displays only the sums or counts of specified data. You can then filter what's displayed in the PivotChart by specifying which values to hide or display.

Row Labels	Sum of Total Sale
A Little Strange, Inc.	$64.00
A1 Catalog	$25.00
Acme Co.	$114.00
Bargain Source	$105.00
Big Bear Supply	$46.00
Northside LLC	$86.00
Sister Brothers, Inc.	$30.00
Super Rich Fizzy Business	$32.00
Westside Liquidators	$218.00
Grand Total	$720.00

1 Set up your PivotTable to display the specific data you want, and position the cursor anywhere within the PivotTable.

2 Select the **Analyze** tab on the Ribbon, go to the **Tools** section, and click the **PivotChart** button.

> **Note**
>
> You also can create a PivotChart directly from the source data by selecting the **Insert** tab and then clicking the **PivotChart** button. With this approach, you have to build the PivotTable/PivotChart field by field, using the PivotTable Fields pane.

3 When the Insert Chart dialog box appears, select the chart type you want and the specific chart in the preview pane. Click **OK** to add the PivotChart to the PivotTable worksheet.

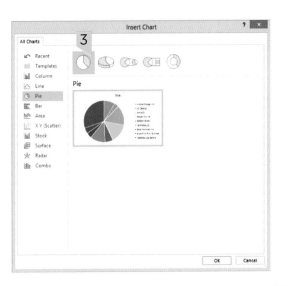

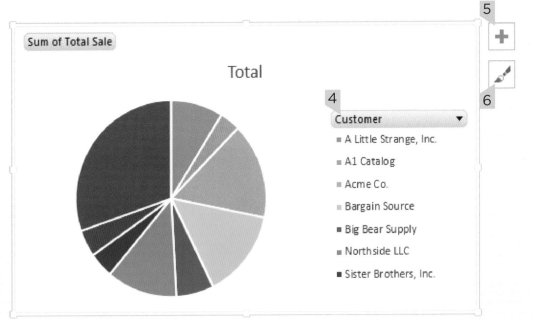

4 To filter the PivotChart, click the field button labeled with the field name, and uncheck those values you don't want displayed.

5 Click the **Chart Elements** (+) button to hide or display various chart elements, such as axis titles, data labels, and the like.

6 Click the **Chart Styles** (*paintbrush*) button to select a different chart style or color scheme. You can also use the controls on the Design tab to further format the chart.

Chapter 13

Analyzing Data

Most worksheets start as raw data, which is then manipulated and formatted to produce useful and presentable results. At times, however, you want to do even more in terms of analyzing the data and even formulating various what-if scenarios.

To this end, Excel includes several what-if analysis tools. The Goal Seek tool lets you set a desired result and manipulate the cells that feed into the formula to give that result. The Scenario Manager lets you create several of these what-if scenarios and compare the results. And the sparkline tool provides instant analysis of trends exhibited by your data.

In This Chapter

- Creating what-if analyses with the Goal Seek tool
- Analyzing multiple what-if scenarios with the Scenario Manager tool
- Comparing multiple scenarios with a scenario summary report
- Using sparklines to highlight data trends

Using Goal Seek for What-If Analysis

When you have a specific result in mind but aren't sure how exactly to get there, use Excel's Goal Seek tool. Goal Seek lets you vary the value in a given cell until the formula that references that cell returns the desired result.

Let's say you're working on your home budget and have created a formula that subtracts all your expenses from your income, thus telling you how much money you have left over at the end of the month. Your what-if scenario involves setting a goal for monthly savings, but you're not quite sure how to accomplish that goal. Use the Goal Seek tool to vary the amount for a given expense, or for your total income (if it truly is variable), and you'll figure out what you need to do to accomplish your savings goal.

	A	B	C	D
1	Income1	$10,000		
2	Income2	$4,000		
3				
4	Housing	$3,000		
5	Auto	$1,000		
6	Groceries	$4,000		
7	Utilities	$2,000		
8	Dining	$1,000		
9	Other	$1,000		
10		1		
11	Savings	$2,000		
12				

Consolidate — What-If Analysis ▾ — Group ▾ — Ungroup ▾

Scenario Manager...

Goal Seek... 2

Data Table...

L	M	N	O	P

1 Select the cell that contains the formula you want to use for your what-if analysis.

2 Select the **Data** tab on the Ribbon, go to the **Data Tools** section, click the **What-If Analysis** button, and click **Goal Seek...**.

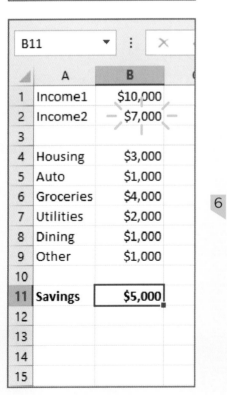

	A	B
1	Income1	$10,000
2	Income2	$4,000
3		
4	Housing	$3,000
5	Auto	$1,000
6	Groceries	$4,000
7	Utilities	$2,000
8	Dining	$1,000
9	Other	$1,000
10		
11	Savings	$2,000
12		
13		
14		
15		

B11

Goal Seek ? ✕

Set cell: B11 ⬛ **3**

4

To value: ⬛

5

By changing cell: ⬛ ⬛

OK   Cancel

3 This displays the Goal Seek dialog box. The formula cell should be referenced in the **Set cell** box; if not, click that cell now to enter it.

4 Enter the target value for the formula into the **To value** box.

5 Determine what cell you want to change to meet your goal, and click that cell in the worksheet to enter it into the **By changing cell** box.

B11

	A	B
1	Income1	$10,000
2	Income2	$7,000
3		
4	Housing	$3,000
5	Auto	$1,000
6	Groceries	$4,000
7	Utilities	$2,000
8	Dining	$1,000
9	Other	$1,000
10		
11	Savings	$5,000
12		
13		
14		
15		

Goal Seek Status ? ✕

Goal Seeking with Cell B11 found a solution.   Step

Target value: 5000   Pause
Current value: $5,000

OK   Cancel

6 Click **OK**, and the Goal Seek tool calculates the necessary value for the cell you set to change. It displays the result in the Goal Seek Status dialog box as well as in your worksheet.

Using Scenario Manager

The Goal Seek tool enables you to perform what-if analysis, one scenario at a time. When you want to evaluate multiple what-if scenarios, use Excel's Scenario Manager tool.

The Scenario Manager lets you specify multiple changes you could make to the data in a formula and then compare the different outcomes. For your home budget, for example, you might create scenarios in which you change your monthly income as well as various expenses to meet a savings goal. Use Scenario Manager to create scenarios for each of these options, and compare them to see which works best for you.

You can also use Scenario Manager to evaluate best-case and worst-case scenarios. For example, if you run a business, you might create scenarios based on different levels of sales in a given week. You can then see what effect the changes in sales have on your bottom line.

Expenses	
Rent	$12,500
Salaries	$16,000
Other	$5,000
Subtotal	$33,500
Profit/Loss	$2,000

① **Select the cell** that contains the formula you want to use for your what-if analysis.

② **Select the Data tab** on the Ribbon, go to the **Data Tools** section, click the **What-If Analysis** button, and click **Scenario Manager…**.

> **Note**
>
> Excel saves each of the scenarios you create. To revisit the scenarios you created for a given worksheet, click **What-If Analysis** and then **Scenario Manager** to reopen the Scenario Manager tool with all your scenarios listed. Note that the last active scenario is the one that remains in your worksheet when you close the Scenario Manager tool.

Scenario Manager

Scenarios:

Fewer Paper Clips
More Widgets
No Taffy
10% Salary Increase

Add...
Delete
Edit...
Merge...
Summary...

Changing cells: $B$10

Comment: Created by Michael Miller on 9/25/2013

Show   Close

Add Scenario

Scenario name:

Changing cells:
B5

Ctrl+click cells to select non-adjacent changing cells.

Comment:
Created by Michael Miller on 9/25/2013

Protection
☑ Prevent changes
☐ Hide

OK   Cancel

3 This displays the Scenario Manager dialog box. Click the **Add...** button to open the Add Scenario dialog box.

4 Enter a name for this scenario into the **Scenario name** box. Enter the cell or range of cells you want to change in this scenario into the **Changing cells** box, or just click to select those cells in your worksheet. Enter any comment on this scenario into the **Comment** box. Click **OK** when you're done.

Scenario Values

Enter values for each of the changing cells.

1:    $B$5   6500

Add   OK   Cancel

Changing cells: $B$10

Comment: Created by Michael Miller on 9/25/2013

Show   Close

5 When the Scenario Values dialog box appears, enter a possible value for the cell(s) you've opted to change, and click **OK**.

6 Repeat steps 3 through 5 to create additional scenarios.

7 Back in the Scenario Manager dialog box, select the scenario you want to view, and click the **Show** button. The values in your worksheet now change to reflect this scenario.

Producing a Scenario Summary Report

After you set up various what-if scenarios using the Scenario Manager, you might want to compare all the possible results. You do this by creating a scenario summary report that displays the results of each scenario you've created, all in a handy spreadsheet table.

1 Open the worksheet that contains the scenarios you previously created. Select the **Data** tab in the Ribbon, go to the **Data Tools** section, click the **What-If Analysis** button, and click **Scenario Manager…**.

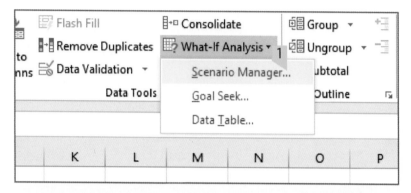

2 This opens the Scenario Manager tool. Click the **Summary…** button to open the Scenario Summary dialog box.

Scenario Summary

	?	×

Report type 3

- ● Scenario summary
- ○ Scenario PivotTable report

Result cells:

B14	

OK	Cancel

3 Check the **Scenario summary** option to create a basic summary report, and click **OK**.

> **Note**
>
> You also can create a PivotTable of your various scenarios. Just click **Scenario PivotTable report** in the Scenario Summary dialog box.

A1	▼	:	×	✓	fx	

	A	B	C	D	E	F	G	H	I	J	K
1											
2		Scenario Summary									
3				Current Values:	Fewer Paper Clips	More Widgets	No Taffy	10% Salary Increase	More Casings		
5		**Changing Cells:**									
6		$B$2		$5,000	$3,000	$5,000	$5,000	$5,000	$5,000		
7		$B$3		$15,000	$15,000	$18,000	$15,000	$15,000	$15,000		
8		$B$4		$9,000	$9,000	$9,000	$0	$9,000	$9,000		
9		$B$10		$16,000	$16,000	$16,000	$16,000	$17,600	$16,000		
10		$B$5		$6,500	$6,500	$6,500	$6,500	$6,500	$8,000		
11		**Result Cells:**									
12		$B$14		$2,000	$0	$5,000	-$7,000	$400	$3,500		
13		Notes: Current Values column represents values of changing cells at									
14		time Scenario Summary Report was created. Changing cells for each									
15		scenario are highlighted in gray.									
16											
17											

4 The resulting scenario summary report highlights the changing cells for each scenario in gray.

Showing Trends with Sparklines

Excel offers another, more visual way to examine your worksheet data, in the form of sparklines. A sparkline is like a mini-chart designed to draw attention trends in your selected data. The sparkline chart is added right next to the data in your worksheet.

1 Use your mouse or keyboard to select the range of cells you want analyzed. These cells should be all in the same row or column.

A	B	C	D	E
Projected Sales				
	2012	2013	2014	2015
North	500,000	550,000	600,000	650,000
South	400,000	425,000	475,000	480,000
East	300,000	320,000	280,000	290,000
West	450,000	500,000	600,000	750,000

2 Select the **Insert** tab on the Ribbon, go to the **Sparklines** section, and select the type of sparkline you want to insert. You can choose from Line, Column, or Win/Loss charts.

REVIEW   VIEW

PivotChart   Line   Column   Win/Loss   Slicer   Timeline   Hy

arts   Sparklines   Filters

F	G	H	I	J	K	L

3 When the Create Sparklines dialog box appears, enter the destination cell for the sparkline into the **Location Range** box, or just highlight the target cell on the worksheet itself. The target cell must be in the same column or row as the cells previously selected. Click **OK** to create the sparkline.

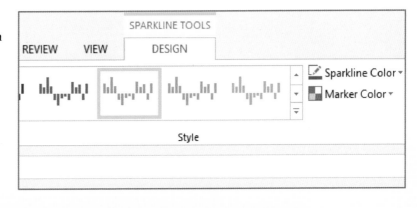

Create Sparklines ? ✕

Choose the data that you want

Data Range: B3:E3

Choose where you want the sparklines to be placed

3

Location Range:

OK   Cancel

4 Excel inserts the sparkline in your worksheet, where you indicated. Repeat steps 1 through 3 to add more sparklines to your worksheet.

B	C	D	E	F
ales				
2012	2013	2014	2015	4
500,000	550,000	600,000	650,000	
400,000	425,000	475,000	480,000	
300,000	320,000	280,000	290,000	
450,000	500,000	600,000	750,000	

5 To format the look of a sparkline, go to the **Design** tab on the Ribbon, and use the tools in the **Style** section. You can select a different Style, Sparkline Color, and Marker Color.

SPARKLINE TOOLS

REVIEW   VIEW   DESIGN

Sparkline Color ▾
Marker Color ▾

Style

> **Note**
>
> The sparkline functions as a background image in the selected cell. This means you can enter text or numbers into the cell and still display the sparkline in addition to what you enter.

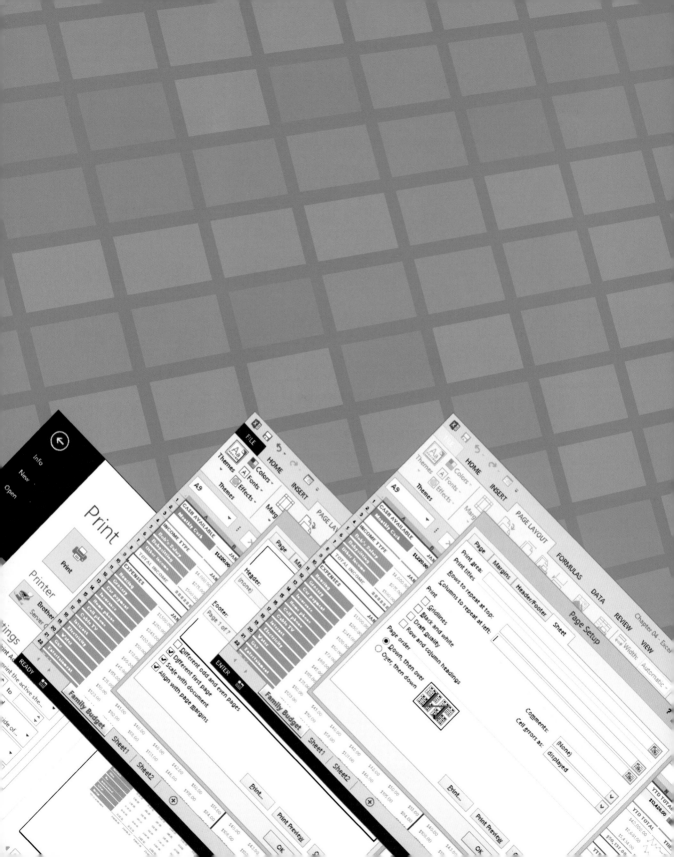

Chapter 14

Printing

Looking at your spreadsheet data on-screen is fine if you're the only one who needs to see it. If you want to share your data, however, in either detailed or summary form, it's a lot easier to pass around printed copies.

Excel enables you to print as much or as little of a given spreadsheet as you like. You can print all the worksheets in a workbook or just a single worksheet that contains summary data. You can even print just a range of cells in a single worksheet, leaving everything else unprinted.

In This Chapter

- Printing a single worksheet or an entire workbook
- Printing a selected print area
- Printing portrait or landscape orientation
- Shrinking a worksheet to print on a single page
- Specifying manual page breaks
- Printing row and column titles across multiple pages
- Printing headers and footers

Printing One or More Worksheets

When it's time to print, you have the option of printing just one worksheet or printing every worksheet in a workbook. It's all a matter of what you select on Excel's Print page.

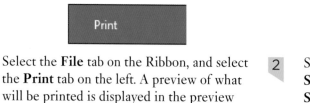

1 Select the **File** tab on the Ribbon, and select the **Print** tab on the left. A preview of what will be printed is displayed in the preview pane.

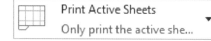

2 Scroll to the **Settings** section, and click the **Selection** control. By default, **Print Active Sheets** is selected; this prints the currently selected worksheet. To instead print all the worksheets in the workbook, click this button, and select **Print Entire Workbook**.

3 To print only selected pages from the worksheet or workbook, use the **Pages** control to select the start and end printed pages. For example, to print just the first page of the current workbook, enter pages **1** to **1**; to print the first two pages, enter pages **1** to **2**.

4 Click the **Printer** button, and select the printer you want to use, if you have more than one available to you.

5 If you want to print more than one copy of the selection, use the **Copies** control to enter the number of copies you want.

6 Click the **Print** button to start printing.

Print

6

🖨
Print

5
Copies: 1 ▲▼

Printer

ⓘ

🖨 Brother MFC-7840W Prin... ▼
Server Offline

Printer Properties

Settings

2

▦ **Print Active Sheets**
Only print the active she... ▼

3

Pages: [ ] ▲▼ to [ ] ▲▼

▤ **Print One Sided**
Only print on one side of... ▼

▤ **Collated**
1,2,3   1,2,3   1,2,3 ▼

▤ **Landscape Orientation** ▼

▯ **Letter**
8.5" x 11" ▼

▭ **Normal Margins** ▼

◀ 1 of 1 ▶

Printing Part of a Worksheet

You don't have to print all the data on a worksheet page. You can specify an area of the worksheet you want to print, and print only that area—essentially ignoring less-important data on that worksheet.

1   Open the worksheet page, and use your mouse or keyboard to select the range of cells you want to print. The range can include cells containing data, charts, and other graphics.

2 Select the **File** tab on the Ribbon, and select the **Print** tab on the left.

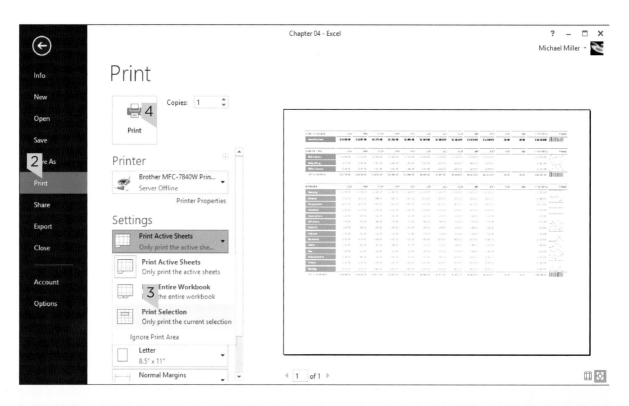

3 Scroll to the **Settings** section, click the **Selection** control, and select **Print Selection**. The selected area now appears in the preview pane.

4 Select the desired printer, number of copies, and other settings, and click the **Print** button to start printing.

Changing Page Orientation

Some spreadsheets fit just fine on a standard 8½ × 11-inch sheet of paper in standard portrait (vertical) orientation. Other spreadsheets are wider than they are tall and display better in landscape (horizontal) orientation. When you're printing, choose the orientation that best fits what you have to print.

1 From the **Print** page, go to the **Settings** section, and click the **Orientation** control.

2 Select **Portrait Orientation** to print taller spreadsheets, or select **Landscape Orientation** to print wider spreadsheets. Verify the print orientation in the print preview section.

Scaling the Spreadsheet to Fit

If the data in a worksheet is too large to fit on a single printed page, you can print it across multiple pages (more on that later) or shrink the print area to better fit the printed page. You can shrink data in several ways. You can shrink all the data onto a single page, shrink the print area so all the columns fit on a single page (with extra rows spreading across multiple pages), or shrink the print area so all the rows fit on a single page (with extra columns spreading across multiple pages).

1 From the **Print** page, go to the **Settings** section, and click the **Scale** control.

2 Select one of the following options: **Fit Sheet on One Page**, **Fit All Columns on One Page**, or **Fit All Rows on One Page**.

Inserting Page Breaks

You can shrink a large worksheet to fit on a single printed page, or you can have that worksheet print across multiple pages instead.

If you choose to print across multiple pages, Excel automatically inserts page breaks where they seem to fit best. Depending on the data in a worksheet, however, these might not be the best spots for page breaks. Fortunately, Excel lets you preview these page breaks and insert your own manual page breaks as necessary.

1 To view the page breaks in a worksheet, select the **View** tab, go to the **Workbook Views** section, and click the **Page Break Preview** button. You now see your worksheet with page breaks added. If you're okay with where the breaks appear, click the **Normal** button on the **View** tab and proceed to printing.

2 To insert a different page break, select the row or column *before* which you want the break to appear.

3 Select the **Page Layout** tab, go to the **Page Setup** section, click the **Breaks** button, and click **Insert Page Break**.

4 To remove a given page break, select the break's row or column, select the **Page Layout** tab, go to the **Page Setup** section, click the **Breaks** button, and click **Remove Page Break**.

5 To remove all page breaks you've inserted into a worksheet and return to the automatic page breaks, select the **Page Layout** tab, go to the **Page Setup** section, click the **Breaks** button, and click **Reset All Page Breaks**.

Configuring Other Print Options

Excel offers several other settings you can use to configure and fine-tune the printed results. You can choose different paper sizes, set wider or narrower margins, opt to print on both sides of the paper, and select different ways to collate multiple pages. All these options are available on the Print page, accessed from the File tab on the Ribbon.

Print One Sided
Only print on one side of...

By default, Excel utilizes one-sided printing. If your printer can print on both sides of the paper, click the **Side** control, and select one of the **Print on Both Sides** options

Collated
1,2,3   1,2,3   1,2,3

By default, Excel prints multiple pages by collating complete sets (pages 1,2,3). If you'd prefer to print all copies of page 1 followed by all copies of page 2, and so on, click the **Collate** control and select **Uncollated**.

Print

Copies: 1

Print

Printer Properties

Settings

Print Active Sheets
Only print the active she...

Pages: to

Print One Sided
Only print on one side of...

Collated
1,2,3   1,2,3   1,2,3

Landscape Orientation

Letter
8.5" x 11"

Normal Margins
Left: 0.7"   Right: 0.7"

No Scaling
Print sheets at their actual...

Page Setup

Letter
8.5" x 11"

To print to a paper size different from the U.S. default of $8\frac{1}{2} \times 11$ inches, click the **Size** control, and select a different paper size.

Normal Margins
Left: 0.7"   Right: 0.7"

To change the margins of the printout, click the **Margins** button, and select either **Wide** or **Narrow**. To set your own custom margins, select **Custom Margins…** to display the Page Setup dialog box, where you can set each of the four margins (top, bottom, left, and right) separately.

Printing Row and Column Titles

If you're printing across multiple pages, you might want to repeat row or column titles on all the printed pages. This helps readers keep their place among all the data.

1 Select the **Page Layout** tab on the Ribbon, go to the **Page Setup** section, and click the **Print Titles** button.

2 This opens the Page Setup dialog box with the Sheet tab selected. Click the **Rows to repeat at top** control, and use your mouse to select one or more title rows in your worksheet. Click the **Columns to repeat at left** control, and use your mouse to select one or more title columns in your worksheet. Click **OK** when you're done, or click **Print...** to go directly to the Print page.

Adding a Header and Footer

You can opt to print headers and footers at the top and bottom of your printed pages. Headers and footers can include basic information about the worksheet—the file name, date created, author, number of pages, and such.

1 Select the **Page Layout** tab on the Ribbon, go to the **Page Setup** section, and click the **Print Titles** button.

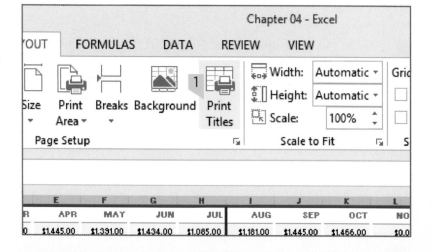

2 This opens the Page Setup dialog box. Select the **Header/Footer** tab. Click the **Custom Header...** button to add a header, or click the **Custom Footer...** button to add a footer.

Header

Header	First Page Header

To format text: select the text, then choose the Format Text button.

To insert a page number, date, time, file path, filename, or tab name: position the insertion point in the edit box, then choose the appropriate button.

To insert picture: press the Insert Picture button. To format your picture, place the cursor in the edit box and press the Format Picture button.

`A` ` ` ` ` ` ` ` ` ` ` ` ` ` ` ` ` ` `

Left section: Center section: Right section:

OK   Cancel

---

3 When the Header or Footer dialog box appears, you can enter different text for the left side, center, and right side of the header or footer. To enter plain text, just type into the appropriate section.

You can enter preformatted fields into any of the three sections as well. Click the appropriate button to enter any of the following: **Page Number**, **Number of Pages**, **Date**, **Time**, **File Path**, **File Name**, or **Sheet Name**. You also can opt to insert a picture, via the **Insert Picture** button.

> **🕑 Tip**
>
> If you want to create a different header or footer for the first page of the printout, select the **First Page Header** or **First Page Footer** tab, and enter the desired text or fields. Click **OK** to insert the header or footer.

Chapter 15

Sharing and Collaborating

Many businesses use spreadsheets for planning purposes—creating budgets, estimates, and the like. This planning often requires input from multiple departments or offices, which means you have a lot of people feeding data into a single workbook.

Microsoft has long recognized the popularity of sharing Excel spreadsheets and has built robust collaborative features into the program. Excel 2013 lets you track changes and include comments from multiple collaborators and share spreadsheet files via email or Microsoft's SkyDrive cloud-based storage service. And if that isn't enough, you can use the Excel Web App to collaborate online—in real time.

In This Chapter

- Sharing a workbook via Microsoft SkyDrive
- Sharing a workbook as an email attachment
- Tracking changes in a shared workbook
- Accepting and rejecting changes from collaborators
- Inserting and reading comments
- Using the Excel Web App to collaborate online

Sharing Online with SkyDrive

Assuming all your collaborators are online (and if they're not, why not?), the easiest way to share an Excel spreadsheet is via Microsoft's SkyDrive cloud-based storage service. When you upload an Excel file to SkyDrive, you can choose who else can access that file and how they can access it—read-only or with full editing privileges.

Your online collaborators can then download the file from SkyDrive to their own computers (and re-upload it when they're done editing), or use the Excel Web App to view and edit the file online, in their web browsers.

1 Open the workbook you want to share, select the **File** tab in the Ribbon, and click the **Share** tab.

2 When the Share screen appears, click **Invite People** and then click the **Save To Cloud** button.

3 When the Save As screen appears, select *Your SkyDrive* in the left column, and navigate to the folder where you want to save the file. When the Save As dialog box appears, enter a name for the file, and click the **Save** button.

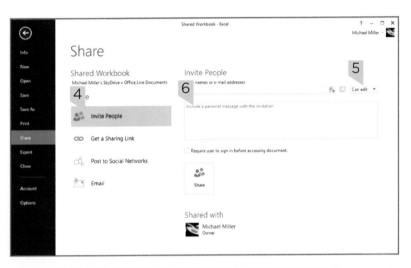

4 You're now returned to the Share screen, with the Invite People panel displayed. Enter the email address of the first person with whom you want to share.

5 Pull down the **Permissions** list beside this person's email address, and select the desired editing level—**Can edit** or **Can view**. (If you select **Can view**, this person can only view the spreadsheet, not make any editing changes.)

6 Enter a message to send to this person, and click the **Share** button. Repeat steps 3 through 6 to share with additional people.

> 🕐 **Tip**
>
> You can also send a link to the shared file via email by clicking the **Email** option on the left. In addition, you can post a link to the shared file on Facebook, Twitter, or LinkedIn by clicking the **Post to Social Networks** option. (If you're posting a public message about this spreadsheet to a social network, you should select **Can view** to limit who can make changes to the file.)

Sharing a Workbook via Email

Some users are more comfortable sharing a spreadsheet the old-fashioned way, by passing the file around via email. When a collaborator receives his copy of the file, he makes his changes and emails the file back to you. You can then accept or reject his changes into your master copy of the spreadsheet (more on that later).

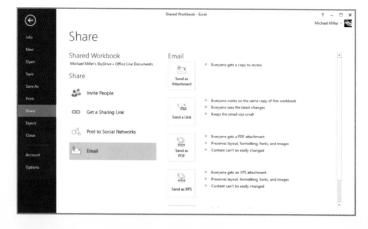

1   Select the **File** tab on the Ribbon, and click the **Share** tab. Click **Email** on the left side of the screen, and click the **Send as Attachment** button on the right.

2   This opens a new, blank email message in your default email program. (Microsoft Outlook is shown in this example.) The workbook file is included as an attachment to the message. Enter your collaborators' email addresses into the **To…** field. Accept the default subject (which is just the file name—probably not too useful) or enter a new subject for the message in the **Subject** field. Enter any accompanying message into the body of the email, and click the **Send** button to send the file via email to the desired recipients.

Enabling Change Tracking

When you share a workbook, each collaborator works on the file on his or her own computer, and uploads or emails the file back to you. You then have to identify each user's changes and decide whether or not to accept them into your master document.

You do this by using Excel's change tracking, which lets you track, display, accept, or reject changes made by each person with whom you've shared the file. You can opt to view the change history directly in the original worksheet or on a separate change history worksheet.

1 You need to turn on sharing and change tracking before you share a workbook with others. Select the **Review** tab, go to the **Changes** section, and click the **Share Workbook** button. When the Share Workbook dialog box opens, select the **Editing** tab, and check the **Allow changes by more than one user at the same time** option. Then select the **Advanced** tab, and choose how long you want to keep the change history (30 days is the default), how often you want changes updated, and how to handle conflicts when more than one user changes the same data (the default is to ask you which changes to accept). Click **OK** when you're done.

2 You now need to enable change tracking. Select the **Review** tab, go to the **Changes** section, click the **Track Changes** button, and click **Highlight Changes**. When the Highlight Changes dialog box opens, check the **Track changes while editing** option. Check **When**, and select either **All** or **Since I last saved**. Check **Who**, and select **Everyone**. To see changes in the worksheet itself, check **Highlight changes on screen**. To list all changes in a separate worksheet, check **List changes on a new sheet**. Click **OK** when you're done. (When you want to stop tracking changes, re-open this dialog box and uncheck the **Track changes while editing** option.)

Accepting and Rejecting Changes

After you've enabled change tracking, you can share the worksheet with your collaborators. When they return their copies of the workbook to you, any cells they've changed are highlighted. You can view who made each change, what type of change it was, when the change was made, and what data was changed. In this way, you control the revisions to the worksheet.

1 All cells that have been revised are flagged in the worksheet. Mouse over each changed cell to see a pop-up note explaining who made the change and what was changed.

2 To accept or reject changes to the worksheet, select the **Review** tab in the Ribbon, go to the **Changes** section, and click **Accept/Reject Changes**. You're prompted to save the workbook before continuing; click **OK**.

> **⚠ Caution**
>
> Not all changes are tracked. Most changes to cell contents are, but formatting changes are not. By default, change history is kept for only the past 30 days; if you have a project that's lasting longer than that, select a longer period to track. If you turn off change tracking, all change history is deleted.

3 When the Select Changes to Accept or Reject dialog box appears, select which changes to examine—when they were made, who made them, and where in the worksheet they were made. Click **OK** to continue.

Select Changes to Accept or Reject   ?   ✕

Which changes
☑ When: Not yet reviewed   ⌄
☐ Who: Everyone   ⌄
☐ Where: [   ] 🔳

           OK   Cancel

4 You now see the Accept or Reject Changes dialog box, with the first change listed. Click to **Accept** or **Reject** this change; the dialog box then displays the next revision in the document. (You also can opt to **Accept All** or **Reject All** changes throughout the entire file.) Click **Close** if you're done.

Accept or Reject Changes   ?   ✕

Change 1 of 3 made to this document:

Michael Miller, 9/27/2013 4:44 PM:

Changed cell G4 from '700' to '725'.

           4

Accept   Reject   Accept All   Reject All   Close

5 In some instances, you might have to choose from two or more values entered into a given cell. In this situation, click the value you want and then click **Accept**. The other change is automatically rejected. Click **Close** when you're done.

Accept or Reject Changes   ?   ✕

Select a value for cell G6:

585 (Original Value)   5
575 (Michael Miller 9/27/2013 16:46)
580 (Michael Miller 9/27/2013 16:48)

Accept   Reject   Accept All   Reject All   Close

Adding Comments

When you're sharing a workbook with others, you might want to leave them comments about some of your work. When they're making their revisions, they might have some comments to leave for you as well.

These comments are not text or data entered into a cell, but rather comments on a cell's existing content. Think of them as digital sticky notes, floating above or beside the cell in question. Comments are only displayed on-screen; they don't print with the worksheet.

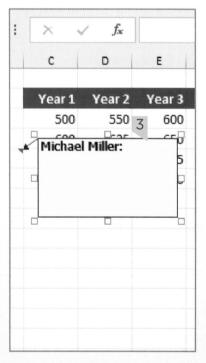

1 To add a comment to a cell, start by selecting that cell in the worksheet.

2 Select the **Review** tab on the Ribbon, go to the **Comments** section, and click the **New Comment** button.

3 This adds a comment box beside the cell, tagged with your name. Click within the comment box to type your comment.

Cells with comments attached have a red flag in the upper-right corner. Hover your mouse over a flagged cell to view its comment.

	A	B	C	D	E	F
			Year 1	Year 2	Year 3	Year 4
		North	500	550	600	650
		East				675
		South				400
		West				550

Michael Miller:
Includes old Southwest region, but not Southeast

Shared Workbook [Shared] - Excel

INSERT   PAGE LAYOUT   FORMULAS   DATA   REVIEW   VIEW

Thesaurus   Translate   Edit Comment   Delete   Previous   Next   Show/Hide Comment   Show All Comments   Show Ink   Protect Sheet W

Language   Comments

fx   South

C	D	E	F	G	H	I	J	K

To delete a comment, select the cell to which the comment is attached, and select the **Review** tab on the Ribbon, go to the **Comments** section, and click the **Delete** button.

You also can choose to display all comments in a worksheet. Select the **Review** tab on the Ribbon, go to the **Comments** section, and click the **Show All Comments** button. Click this button again to hide all comments.

Collaborating Online with the Excel Web App

When you have multiple collaborators who need to work on a spreadsheet in real time, the best approach is to collaborate online with the Excel Web App. When you and your collaborators edit a file with the Excel Web App, changes made by one user are immediately reflected on the other users' screens. When one person changes the data in a cell, all the other online users see it as it happens. This enables everyone to react much more quickly to revisions and move the project along at a faster pace.

Using the Excel Web App to collaborate on shared files is much faster than sharing and editing files via email. It also means you don't have to worry about accepting or rejecting changes; all revisions happen on-screen in real time. When somebody makes a change, you see it and can react to it immediately.

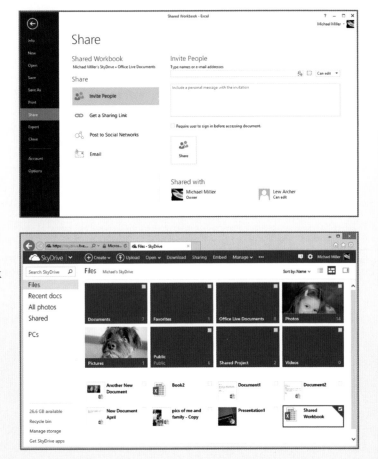

1. Start by uploading the worksheet to SkyDrive and sharing it with the other collaborators on your team.

2. Open SkyDrive in your web browser (skydrive.live.com), navigate to the shared file, and click to open it.

The following is a screenshot showing the Microsoft Excel Web App interface:

Browser tabs: https://skydrive.live.... | Micros... | Shared Workbook.xlsx - Mic... ×

SkyDrive ▸ Shared Workbook.xlsx   Microsoft Excel Web App   Michael Miller   Sign out ?

Ribbon tabs: FILE HOME INSERT DATA VIEW X OPEN IN EXCEL SHARE

Ribbon buttons: Paste, Cut, Copy (Clipboard) | Calibri 11, B I U D, A (Font) | Wrap Text, Merge & Center (Alignment) | ABC 123, Number Format (Number) | Survey, Sort & Filter as Table (Tables) | Insert, Delete (Cells) | AutoSum, Clear, Sort, Find (Editing)

fx 400

	A	B	C	D	E	F	G	H	I	J	K	L	M	N	O	P	Q	R
1																		
2			Year 1	Year 2	Year 3	Year 4	Year 5											
3		North	500	550	600	650	700											
4		East	600	625	650	675	725											
5		South	400	430	425	400	400											
6		West	300	400	450	550	580											

Sheet tabs: Shared | RSVP Tracker | Sheet1 | Sheet2 | Sheet4 | Sheet5 | Sheet6 | Sheet7 | ⊕

2 PEOPLE EDITING ▾

3 This displays the workbook in the Excel Web App in your web browser. Edit the workbook as necessary. The changes you make are instantly applied to the online file. Anyone else currently working on the workbook sees the changes as you make them—just as you see the changes they make.

4 If someone else is also editing this workbook online, you see a message in the lower-right corner of the window. Click this message to see who's online.

Lew Archer
Michael Miller
2 PEOPLE EDITING ▾

Appendix A

Glossary

absolute reference   A cell or range reference that refers to cells by their fixed position in the worksheet. The reference does not change when a formula is copied to another location. It's identified by a number sign ($) in front of the row and/or column identifiers.

active cell   The currently selected cell in a worksheet.

area chart   A variation of the line chart, where the area between the line and the X axis is filled in with color to indicate volume.

Auto Fill   A feature that automatically extends data into cells based on the pattern of data in preceding cells.

AutoSum   An automatic application of the SUM function, used to total the contents of preceding cells.

axis   One of two (in a 2-D chart) or three (in a 3-D chart) lines that border the chart area and provide a reference for measurement.

cell   The unique intersection of a row and column in a worksheet into which data is entered.

chart   The graphic representation of data in a worksheet.

column   A vertical group of cells in a worksheet, identified by a letter.

data series   In a chart, the column, bar, or other graphical element that represents a data value.

data table   A table of numerical values displayed alongside the graphical representation of those values in a chart.

field   A category of data in a database, data form, or table.

Flash Fill   A feature that automatically enters data into selected cells based on examples in a worksheet.

formula   An equation that performs certain calculations in a worksheet. In Excel, all formulas begin with the equals sign (=).

Formula bar   The part of the Excel window, located between the Ribbon and the spreadsheet grid, that displays the value of the currently selected cell. You can enter and edit cell data from the Formula bar as well.

function   A predefined formula built into Excel.

Goal Seek   A what-if analysis tool that enables users to find a specified value for a given cell by adjusting the value of another cell.

gridline   In a worksheet, the vertical and horizontal lines that extend down and across the worksheet, defining the borders of columns and rows. In a chart, these are the lines that extend up or across the plot area from each major tick mark.

legend   A box displayed on a chart that identifies the colors or patterns assigned to each data series or category in the chart.

Microsoft Excel Web App The online version of the Excel spreadsheet program, accessible with any web browser via Microsoft SkyDrive.

Microsoft SkyDrive Microsoft's cloud-based online storage service.

number format A specific way in which numbers are displayed in a cell. Excel offers a multitude of number formats, including currency, percentage, date, and time formats.

operator Those symbols, such as + and –, used to perform mathematical calculations.

PivotChart The graphical representation of data in a PivotTable that itself is interactive.

PivotTable A type of interactive table that can display the selected data in different ways by manipulating the rows and columns of the table.

Quick Access Toolbar The customizable small toolbar in the upper-left corner of the Excel window.

Quick Analysis A feature that enables single-click access to formatting and analysis of selected data.

range A grouping of two or more cells in a worksheet.

record A collection of data about a given subject. Each record contains multiple fields as defined by the database or table.

reference A means of identifying the location of a cell or range of cells in a worksheet. In Excel, a cell reference consists of the cell's column letter and row number.

Ribbon The user interface (in Excel and other Microsoft Office programs) that groups commands for related tasks in tabs that run across the upper part of the program window.

row A horizontal group of cells in a worksheet, identified by number.

Scenario Manager A what-if analysis tool that enables users to create sets of different input values that produce different calculated results.

SmartArt A type of interactive graphic that automatically creates diagrams based on text input.

sparkline A small chart that visually presents trends in the selected data.

spreadsheet A type of computer application in which data arranged in a grid of rows and columns can be manipulated and used in calculations.

table In Excel, a range of cells that express database-like data as a series of records (rows) and fields (columns).

template A predesigned workbook with visual formatting and built-in formulas used as a pattern for creating new workbooks.

text box A rectangular object in a worksheet into which you can enter and display text.

trendline A line, superimposed on the elements of a chart, that depicts trends in the underlying data.

WordArt A graphics tool for creating visually sophisticated text elements.

workbook An Excel file that contains one or more worksheets.

worksheet The primary document used to store and work with data within an Excel file. Each tab in a workbook is an individual worksheet.

X-axis The axis that runs horizontally along the bottom of a chart; also called the category axis.

Y-axis The axis that runs vertically along the side of a chart; also called the value axis.

Appendix B

Keyboard Shortcuts

Description	Shortcut Keys
Add nonadjacent cell or range to current selection using arrow keys	Shift+F8
Add more values to active column using data surrounding that column	Ctrl+E
Add or edit cell comment	Shift+F2
Calculate all worksheets in all open workbooks	F9
Calculate active worksheet	Shift+F9
Cancel current entry	Esc
Clear contents of active cell	Backspace
Close open menu, submenu, dialog box, or message window	Esc
Close selected workbook	Ctrl+W
Complete cell entry and select cell above	Shift+Enter
Complete cell entry and select current cell	Enter
Control menu	Alt+Spacebar
Copy formula from cell above selected cell into cell	Ctrl+'
Copy selected cell(s)	Ctrl+C
Copy value from cell above selected cell into cell	Ctrl+Shift+"
Create chart from selected data in separate Chart sheet	F11
Create embedded chart from selected data	Alt+F1
Create Table dialog box	Ctrl+L or Ctrl+T
Currency number format	Ctrl+Shift+$
Current date	Ctrl+;
Current time	Ctrl+Shift+:
Cut selected cells	Ctrl+X
Date number format	Ctrl+Shift+#

Description	Shortcut Keys
Delete dialog box	Ctrl+-
Display menu or message for Error Checking button	Alt+Shift+F10
Display outline symbols	Ctrl+8
Display shortcut menu for selected item	Shift+F10
Edit Hyperlink dialog box	Ctrl+K
Exit full-screen mode	Esc
Extend mode toggle	F8
Extend selection by one cell	Shift+arrow key
Extend selection of cells to last nonblank cell in same column or row	Ctrl+Shift+arrow key
Extend selection of cells to last used cell on worksheet	Ctrl+Shift+End
Extend selection to beginning of worksheet	Ctrl+Shift+Home
Fill Down	Ctrl+D
Fill Right	Ctrl+R
Fill selected cell range with current entry	Ctrl+Enter
Find	Ctrl+F
Format Cells dialog box	Ctrl+1
Format Cells dialog box, with Font tab selected	Ctrl+Shift+F
Formula Bar, expand or collapse	Ctrl+Shift+U
Function Arguments dialog box	Ctrl+A
General number format	Ctrl+Shift+~
Go To dialog box	Ctrl+G or F5
Help pane	F1
Hide or display objects	Ctrl+6
Hide selected columns	Ctrl+0
Hide selected rows	Ctrl+9
Insert new worksheet into workbook	Shift+F11
Insert dialog box	Ctrl+Shift++ (plus sign)
Insert Function dialog box	Shift+F3
Insert Hyperlink dialog box	Ctrl+K
Insert contents of Clipboard at insertion point and replace any selection	Ctrl+V

Description	Shortcut Keys
Maximize or restore selected workbook window	Ctrl+F10
Minimize workbook window	Ctrl+F9
Move one cell to right	Tab
Move one screen down	PgDn
Move one screen left	Alt+PgUp
Move one screen right	Alt+PgDn
Move one screen up	PgUp
Move to beginning of current row	Home
Move to beginning of worksheet	Ctrl+Home
Move to edge of current data region	Ctrl+arrow key
Move to next sheet in workbook	Ctrl+PgDn
Move to previous cell	Shift+Tab
Move to last cell on worksheet	Ctrl+End
Move to previous sheet in workbook	Ctrl+PgUp
Next tab in dialog box	Ctrl+Tab
Next workbook window	Ctrl+F6
Next worksheet tab	Ctrl+PgDn
Normal view	Alt+W+L
Number format	Ctrl+Shift+!
Open dialog box	Ctrl+O
Open selected cell for editing	F2
Outline border to selected cell(s)	Ctrl+Shift+&
Page Break Preview view	Alt+W+I
Page Layout view	Alt+W+P
Paste	Ctrl+V
Paste Name dialog box	F3
Paste Special dialog box	Ctrl+Alt+V
Percentage number format	Ctrl+Shift+%
Previous tab in dialog box	Ctrl+Shift+Tab

Description	Shortcut Keys
Previous worksheet tab	Ctrl+PgUp
Print preview display on Print tab	Ctrl+F2
Print tab	Ctrl+P
Quick Analysis options for selected cells	Ctrl+Q
Recheck dependent formulas and calculate all cells in all open workbooks	Ctrl+Alt+Shift+F9
Remove cell contents from selected cells without affecting cell formats or comments	Delete
Remove outline border	Ctrl+Shift+_
Repeat last command or action	F4 or Ctrl+Y
Replace	Ctrl+H
Restore window size of selected workbook window	Ctrl+F5
Ribbon, display or hide	Ctrl+F1
Save active file with its current file name, location, and file format	Ctrl+S
Scientific number format	Ctrl+Shift+^
Select all cells that contain comments	Ctrl+Shift+O
Select entire column in worksheet	Ctrl+Spacebar
Select entire row in worksheet	Shift+Spacebar
Select current and next sheets in workbook	Ctrl+Shift+PgDn
Select current and previous sheets in workbook	Ctrl+Shift+PgUP
Select current region around selected cell	Ctrl+Shift+*
Select current region if a worksheet contains data	Ctrl+A
Select entire worksheet	Ctrl+Shift+Spacebar
Size command	Ctrl+F8
Start new line in same cell	Alt+Enter
Time number format	Ctrl+Shift+@
Undo	Ctrl+Z

Index

data series (charts), 210, 300

Data tab, 3

data tables (charts), 206, 300

date and time functions, 175

dates, 29-29

decimal numbers, entering, 27

decimal places, displaying, 61

deleting
- cell data, 34-35
- cells, single, 86-87
- cells *versus* cell content, 86
- columns, 83
- columns containing data, 82
- copying ranges and, 148
- ranges, 150-151
- rows, 82
- rows containing data, 82
- tables, 233
- worksheets, 115

dialog boxes
- Accept or Reject Changes, 295
- Change Chart Type, 191
- Choose a SmartArt Graphic, 218-219
- Create New Theme Colors, 133
- Create Sparkline, 273
- Custom Views, 14-15
- Edit Series, 193
- Error Checking, 173
- Excel Options, 16-17
- Find and Replace, 36-37
- Format Cells, 29
- Function Arguments, 177
- Goal Seek, 267
- Insert, 85
- Insert Chart, 187, 263
- Insert Function, 177
- Insert Pictures, 214-215
- Move Chart, 189
- Move or Copy, 110
- New Name, 77
- Page Special, 39
- Recommended PivotTables, 247
- Save As, 11
- Scenario Values, 269
- Select Data Source, 192
- Style, 67
- Value Field Settings, 253
- Zoom, 15

distributed alignment, 51

division (/) operator, 161

Draw Border option, 69

E

Edit Series dialog box, 193

editing
- cell data, 32-33
- change tracking, 293
- copying cells, 38-39
- date formatting, 29
- deleting cell data, 34-35
- Find & Select button, 36-37
- formulas, 164-165
- moving cells, 40-41
- numbers as text, 31
- replacing text, 36-37
- time formatting, 29

email, workbook sharing, 292

engineering functions, 175

entering data, 23
- dates, 28-29
- fractions, 27
- numbers, 26-27
- tables, 228-229
- text, 30-31
- times, 28-29

entering formulas, 162

equal to (=) operator, 161

equals sign (=) in formulas, 162, 174

Error Checking dialog box, 173

error checking formulas, 173

Excel Options dialog box, 16-17

Excel Web app, 301
- collaboration and, 298-299
- Formula bar, 4
- Ribbon, 4
- Ribbon tabs, 4
- SkyDrive, 290-291
- worksheet, 4
- Worksheet tab, 4

exponentiation (^) operator, 161

extracting data, 155

F

fields, 250-251, 300

File tab, blank spreadsheets, 7

files
- opening, 12-13
- uploading to SkyDrive, 5

fill color, 56-57

filtering data
- PivotTables, 256-261
- tables, 235

financial functions, 175

Find & Select button, 36-37

Find and Replace dialog box, 36-37

Flash Fill, 154-155, 300

fonts, 44-45
- changing, 46-47
- color, 45
- size, 46-47
- workbooks, 134-135

footers, printing, 286-287

Format Cells dialog box, 29

Format Painter, 71

formats
- automatic number formats, 62-63
- numbers, 58-59

formatting, 43
- 3-D rotation (charts), 209
- Accounting Number, 60
- axes (charts), 202
- axis titles (charts), 203
- bold, 44-45
- chart area, 200
- chart elements, 198-199
- clearing, 44
- columns, 98-99
- conditional, 64-65
- copying between worksheets, 130
- copying cell formatting, 70-71
- currency, 60-61
- data labels (charts), 205
- data series (charts), 210

referenced worksheets in formulas, 170-171

references, 301

reformatting columns, 155

relative cell references, 166

renaming
  tabs, 17
  worksheets, 113

replacing
  data, 88, 90-91, 146
  text, 36-37

resizing charts, 188

Review tab, 3

Ribbon, 2, 301
  adding commands, 17
  adding tabs, 17
  customizing, 16-17
  hiding, 17
  removing commands, 17
  reordering, 17
  Web app, 4

Ribbon tabs, 2
  Add-Ins, 21
  Advanced, 21
  Customize Ribbon, 21
  Data, 3
  Formulas, 3, 21
  General, 21
  Home, 3
  Insert, 3
  Language, 21
  Page Layout, 3
  Proofing, 21
  Quick Access Toolbar, 21
  renaming, 17
  Review, 3
  Save, 21
  Trust Center, 21
  View, 3, 14-15
  Web app, 4

right alignment, 49

rotating text, 54-55

rotation, 3-D charts, 209

row headers, 74, 126

rows, 24, 73, 301
  copying, 88-89
  deleting, 82
  deleting with data, 82
  formatting, 98-99
  freezing, 94-95
  height, 79
  hiding, 92
  inserting, 80
  moving, 90-91
  naming, 76-77
  selecting, 75
  tables, removing, 230-231
  titles, printing, 285
  unhiding, 93

S

Save As dialog box, 11, 291

Save As option, 10-11

Save Current Theme dialog box, 137

Save tab, 21

saving
  to cloud, 10-11
  spreadsheets, 10-11

scaling for printing, 281

scatter charts, 185

Scenario Manager, 265, 268-269, 301
  scenario summary report, 270-271

Scenario Values dialog box, 269

screen, hiding elements, 15

Select Data Source dialog box, 192

shapes, inserting, 220-221

sharing, 289. *See also* collaboration
  SkyDrive, 290-291
  workbooks, email, 292

Sheet Options, 126

shortcuts. *See* keyboard shortcuts

Show (View tab), 15

showing
  column headers, 126
  formulas, 172
  gridlines, 125
  row headers, 126

size, fonts, 46-47

SkyDrive, 5, 301
  opening files, 13
  saving to, 11
  sharing and, 290-291
  uploading files, 5

slicers (PivotTables), 256-257

SmartArt, 218-219, 301

sorting
  basic sort, 100
  custom sort, 101-103
  PivotTables, 255
  tables, 234

source data
  charts, changing, 192-193
  PivotTables, changing, 254

(space) intersection operator, 161

sparklines, 272-273, 301

splitting cells, merged, 97

spreadsheets, 301
  blank, 6-7
  cells, 24-25
  column headers, 74
  column insertion, 81
  column selection, 75
  columns, 24
  navigation keyboard shortcuts, 25
  new, 6-7
  opening, 12-13
  range naming, 142-143
  ranges, 139
  row deletion, 82
  row headers, 74
  row insertion, 80
  row selection, 75
  rows, 24
  saving, 10-11
  templates, 6-9

statistical functions, 175

stock charts, 185

storage, SkyCloud, 5

Style dialog box, 67

styles
  cells, 66
  cells, new, 67

charts, 196-197

    tables, applying, 238-239

subtraction (-) operator, 161

SUM function, 252

surface charts, 185

T

tables, 225, 301. *See also* PivotTables

    columns, 232-233, 236

    converting to normal range, 237

    data, 228-229, 235

    ranges, converting, 226-227

    rows, removing, 230-231

    sorting, 234

    styles, applying, 238-239

tabs. *See also* Ribbon tabs

    color, 114

templates, 6-9, 301

text

    alignment, 48-51

    bold, 44-45

    centering across multiple columns, 53

    entering, 30-31

    fonts, 44-45

    italic, 44-45

    orientation, 55

    rotating, 54-55

    vertical, 55

    wrapping with cells, 52

text boxes, 222, 301

text functions, 175

text (&) operator, 161

theme effects, 131

themes, workbooks, 136-137

time, 28-29

timelines, PivotTables, 258-259

titles

    axes, formatting, 203

    charts, formatting, 204

    printing, 285

toolbar, Quick Access toolbar, 2, 18-19

totaling columns, 236

tracking changes, 293

    accepting, 294-295

    rejecting, 294-295

trendlines, 301

Trust Center tab, 21

typing information. *See* data entry; entering data

U–V

unhiding

    columns, 93

    rows, 93

    worksheets, 120-121

union (,) operator, 161

uploading to SkyDrive, 5

Value Field Settings dialog box, 253

vertical text, 55

View controls, 2

View tab, 3, 14-15

    Show, 15

views

    changing, 14-15

    Custom Views, 14-15

    Page Break Preview, 14-15

visual effect, workbooks, 131

W

Web app. *See* Excel Web app

web functions, 175

Web-based apps, 5

what-if analysis

    Goal Seek and, 266-267

    Scenario Manager, 268-269

WordArt, 223, 301

workbooks, 301

    Blank workbook tile, 6

    color, 132-133

    copying worksheets to, 112

    fonts, 134-135

    moving worksheets to, 112

    names, managing, 145

    overview, 106-107

    printing, 276

    Recent workbooks, 13

    sharing via email, 292

    theme effects, 131

    themes, applying, 136-137

    visual effects, 131

Worksheet tab, 2, 4

worksheets, 2, 301. *See also* spreadsheets

    background color, 127

    background picture, 128-129

    copying, 110

    copying to different workbook, 112

    creating, 108

    default number, 109

    deleting, 115

    formatting, copying between, 130

    formula references, 170-171

    gridline color, 124

    gridlines, hiding/showing, 125

    grouping, 116-117

    hiding/unhiding, 120-121

    moving, 111

    moving to different workbook, 112

    overview, 106-107

    page breaks, 282-283

    panes, 118-119

    printing multiple, 276-277

    printing parts, 278-279

    printing to fit, 281

    renaming, 113

    tab color, 114

    Web app, 4

wrapping text within cells, 52

X-Y-Z

X axis (charts), 194, 301

Y axis (charts), 194, 301

Zoom dialog box, 15

zooming, 15